MISFITS
WELCOME

MISFITS

FIND YOURSELF IN JESUS AND BRING

WELCOME

THE WORLD ALONG FOR THE RIDE

MATTHEW BARNETT

NELSON
BOOKS

An Imprint of Thomas Nelson

Published in Nashville, Tennessee, by Nelson Books, an imprint of Thomas Nelson. Nelson Books and Thomas Nelson are registered trademarks of HarperCollins Christian Publishing, Inc.

Published in association with the literary agency of The Fedd Agency, Inc., Post Office Box 341973, Austin, Texas 78734.

Thomas Nelson titles may be purchased in bulk for educational, business, fund-raising, or sales promotional use. For information, please e-mail SpecialMarkets@ ThomasNelson.com.

ISBN: 978-0-7180-2190-0 (IE)

**The Library of Congress Cataloging-in-Publication Data
is on file with the Library of Congress**

ISBN-978-1-4002-0656-8

Printed in the United States of America

14 15 16 17 18 RRD 6 5 4 3 2 1

CONTENTS

INTRODUCTION

One of the best days of my life was when I drove my little Nissan Sentra from my sheltered life in Phoenix, Arizona, as a megachurch pastor's son to the heart of downtown Los Angeles to help my father with his first church in the City of Angels. I was only twenty, but I was the acting pastor! Totally out of my element. I was unprepared, unqualified, and really unsure. Why did I say this was the best day? Because it was the day I truly needed God. The day I realized I couldn't figure life out on my own.

The streets of Los Angeles did not operate like those in Phoenix. A neighborhood decimated by crime was not what I had in mind. I thought I was just moving to Los Angeles for a few months until my dad could find a real pastor. Little did I realize I would later commit the rest of my life to this city. Nothing here functioned like the church where I was raised.

I figured I would be able to usher in rapid growth at my new church. It's in my blood; I'm the third generation of megachurch pastors in my family. Instead, I was about to experience megashock. I always blended in with ease back home. Not now, not here. I was totally alone, full of fear, and out of ideas.

For the first time in my life, I did not belong. I was a misfit! A pastor's kid who thought he had it all together was now a young man trying to make it through one night in this strange new city. The sights, the sounds, the diversity, the pockets of great poverty. A city truly mixed with potential, hope, and despair. Cardboard boxes of homeless people underneath the corporate skyline. Promise and sadness merged together in a feeling of unease.

It's amazing how life can pivot. One day you feel like you are controlling the flow of life. You seem to manage it perfectly. Then, *wham!* you have no idea how to make it through a night. This was my dilemma, my start, my transformation. My entire life I thought I knew what a misfit was. But overnight I had become one. All my self-confidence had been ripped from me. I had to start over. But starting over isn't always bad—especially when Christ becomes the center of the rebuilding.

Can you remember a time in your childhood when you feared going to school because you did not fit in? Have you ever looked in the mirror and were ashamed of the person you saw? Is the dream in your heart bigger than your skill set? Are you in a place in your life that does not make sense? Maybe you're in a season of recent devastation, and pain seems to have become your identity.

Have you ever felt like a misfit? Just saying the word *misfit* seems to strike a nerve. The truth is, in many ways, we all feel like misfits. We just don't fit into the pattern and flow of life. But that's where things get interesting. In fact, the unknown, the things unseen, is where miracles happen.

■

One thing I've realized is that being different doesn't disqualify you from a dynamic life. It prepares you. The goal of this book is to get you to see that living out of the box isn't always a bad thing. Embracing the misfit in you is the open door to a very exciting journey.

The Bible is full of stories of misfits. A little shepherd boy named David took on a giant with a slingshot. Common fishermen became disciples. You might remember the Sunday school flannel board and the teacher who told dramatic stories about underdogs who did mighty things. We marvel that the Bible is full of misfits, and maybe that is what makes the stories so powerful. Think about David or Daniel or Peter or Paul. They embraced their inner misfits. So why don't we?

Even though we can celebrate the underdog in the Bible, we often hide from the fact that God is looking for that same quality in us. He's looking for people who don't have it all together but are willing to let God take their lives and run with them. What if we can be those kinds of people? What if we can use our unqualified status as the start to bigger dreams and a life of redemption? That's the desire of this book.

My passion is that we will look in the mirror, see who we are, and embrace it so we can progress down the road of life. There are dreams to be dreamed through the process of being a misfit, and those dreams lead us and others toward redemption. James 1:23–25 describes the Word of God as a mirror.

> Anyone who listens to the word but does not do what it says is like someone who looks at his face in a mirror and, after looking at himself, goes away and immediately forgets what he looks like. But whoever looks intently into the perfect law that gives freedom, and continues in it—not forgetting what they have heard, but doing it—they will be blessed in what they do.

God wants us to look into the mirror of His Word so that we can know exactly who we are. The Word of God shows us not only who we are, but what we can become. What happens when we look at our lives and measure them up to His Word? We realize we fall short. Romans 3:23 says, "For all have sinned and fall short of the glory of God." The reflection of the Word of God shows us the blemishes, the hypocrisy, the million ways we seem to miss the target.

Even though we miss the mark, God's incredible love uses us despite the fact we fall short. The standard reveals how much God uses us despite ourselves. He loves us even when we don't like the person we see. Then, by His grace He uses us in our weakness as a gift to the world. Grace. It inspires us to use our weakness to make a difference.

The mirror of God's Word exposes the misfits that we are. It exposes our selfishness, our flesh, and our wandering ways. It exposes our incredible shortcomings. But we have a choice: we can be inspired by the challenge to become more, or be crushed by how far we have to go. Can we be honest? It hurts when we see the misfit in us compared to God's standard. In spite of it, God shows us who we are out of His incredible love. He reminds us just how much He loves to use misfits who surrender their will to His perfect plan. God is not looking to use a perfect person, but rather the fully surrendered one.

We live in a world that likes to play the "Gotcha" game—to catch people in their lies and look for a way to trap others in their inconsistencies. We see it in politics, celebrity life, and everyday family encounters. Humans often reveal the weaknesses of others in order to expose and shame one another. God, on the other hand, wants to show us our weaknesses—who we really are—so He can take us somewhere brand-new. Being honest about being a misfit is the open door to usefulness. God is not interested in our perfection as much as our vulnerability.

■

As we take the journey together, we are going to see that God is actively looking for misfits. "Do not be conformed to this world, but be transformed by the renewing of your mind," the Bible says in Romans 12:2 (NASB). God is looking for people who don't think like everyone else to submit their lives, circumstances, or whatever they have left to fulfill His calling.

I remember years ago when my father took me to a library in Phoenix to study all the great people God had used in history—Billy Sunday, Martin Luther King Jr., Mother Teresa, Charles Spurgeon, and other famous historical figures. I realized that every single one of these people had one thing in common: they were labeled misfits. When they embraced their calling, even in the midst of their own struggles, they were misunderstood. What encouraged me the most was that they came to terms with the simple fact that they were different, and they were okay with it.

In fact, some of the people I read about were making society better even though they were continual works in progress. They were greatly flawed and yet being used. Then I realized that God can do more with people who take off their masks and embrace their misfit status than people who hide behind safety.

Life begins when we remove the mask of trying to make life happen and allow God to break us in our vulnerability. Embracing how God can use anything for His glory is a very encouraging step toward becoming a dreamer who leads others toward redemption.

Everyone has something to give God. If you feel like a failure because of your past, give Him your past. If you feel like the calling is beyond your ability, give God your inability. If you feel defeated because of a sudden setback, give God your total determination. We always have something to give God, and everything is big—even the small stuff—when we give it to God.

I know from experience that embracing my own misfit status as a pastor healed me. I stopped forcing myself to live under the false banner of being perfect or having it all together. Simply put, I had nothing left. I had no safe church to fall back on. My family was four hundred miles away, and I was only one year removed from my teenage years. A misfit pastor. It was hard to admit my incapable status, but it was a glorious revelation—like pushing the reset button on life. I think that's true for everybody.

This book is a reflection of the journey and process of moving from that place to finding God's dream. It's also one big welcome mat to celebrate people who feel like misfits. This book is for those who feel brokenhearted, discouraged, or degraded, who suddenly find themselves in a new era of life where the surroundings look unfamiliar.

Maybe you feel all alone and suddenly life doesn't go according to design. Maybe you have felt like a square peg all your life and you are looking for a defining moment. Maybe the mistakes of yesterday have tried to define tomorrow's future. Let's walk down this road together with honesty, openness, and hope in God's power to use us misfits.

■

I am writing this part of the book on the eighth floor of the former Queen of Angels Hospital—now known as the Dream Center. It's a church that functions as a 24-7 spiritual hospital full of hundreds of people who have defied the odds: people labeled addicts, prostitutes who are now moving forward into a glorious future, lost kids, and lost souls.

This was not my perfect plan. It wasn't even a concept when I came here at the age of twenty, but another twenty years later, it is a direct result of telling God that I was a misfit and I needed help. "God, I don't understand how to reach this city." But God understood. He decided I needed a hospital to help the misfits of our city.

The pages of this book contain many of their stories and the principles of change that have helped them move from misfits to dreamers to redeemers. I hope you will allow me to share my journey with you and show you the beautiful outcome of this surrendered misfit.

one

THE MISFIT IN US ALL

U niqueness is a powerful thing. It's a wonderful thing. The thing we often think is a liability to the world is the very thing God can use to change it.

Right now focus on the greatest liability you think you have. Not smart enough, not talented enough, not creative enough. Stop right there! If you feel disqualified—in any way—to be used by God, then you need to know right now that your feelings of inadequacy are actually a qualification of usefulness. The Bible is a book of misfits. It's what intrigues us, inspires us, and allows us to see God at work through people who were totally unqualified. We can often identify with people's failures even more than their success.

Everything about my life screams, "Misfit!" The neighborhood where I pastor had been abandoned for years. I came right after the 1992 Los Angeles riots, so things were still very intense. Also, many churches had moved out of the urban community for the safety of the suburbs, creating a void in the community. At any given moment there were more people in the bathroom at the church my father pastored in Phoenix than there were in my entire church on a great day.

"God, I can't do this! I can't relate. I don't have any experience with the needs of this community. Why did You send me to the one place where I have no foundational knowledge of what to do?"

I hated that about my life then.

"Why did You send me, God, to a place where I clearly don't understand the culture, poverty, or community?"

But then God began to speak to me: *I didn't call you to the inner city to be relevant, but to be revolutionary. You can honor Me in a greater way by being simply available than if everything came easily for you.*

When I showed up in this city of millions, I had it all planned out. I would preach great sermons and people would come to hear me. If I could just do things perfectly, God could use me to build a great church. There was only one problem. *God never wanted that.* He didn't want my perfection. He wanted my availability.

I struggled for years trying to figure out if momentum would ever come my way. Have you ever felt that way? That the wind is constantly in your face, in the face of your family, and in the face of the vision God has given you? It's a dangerous place, a sad place, and it can sometimes feel endless. It took me five years being a failure of a pastor to realize that God never wanted my perfect plans. He wanted me, the imperfect me.

Brokenness is the greatest gift we can give God. It's a gift that God can work with; it's a gift that moves His heart.

One day I stopped trying to figure out how to *crack the code* of reaching a city and realized it was time for God to *crack me open* and reveal the beautiful rough edges that were in me. What I found was beyond astonishing. I began to discover that embracing the unknown in myself was a wonderful thing that unleashed creativity and vision.

Embracing our misfit status is realizing we don't have to be perfect to be used—just willing to be uniquely who God made us. Life doesn't have to be predictable to be wonderful.

Often there are quirks about our lives that we see as weaknesses or even embarrassments. Maybe it's a big personality that dominates a room; maybe it's a quiet personality in the midst of a big room. Maybe it's a discouraging past that won't let you go; maybe it's a future that seems elusive. Maybe it's taking on a task that is greater than your understanding.

In my case it was being a kid from Phoenix who had no clue how to reach the cold, urban streets of Los Angeles. One night changed all that. I decided I would give God my inabilities and allow Him to reshape this flawed kid with no street ministry experience. I presented my clueless self to God, and in the middle of rock bottom I discovered rock bottom is not where people go to die but where people go to be recreated.

Suddenly I didn't have to figure out how to get through my limitations. I decided being out of my comfort zone was perfectly fine. The greatest prayer I prayed was, "God, use this kid who has no idea what he's doing."

God delighted in the fact that He had a young man who didn't have it all together but was flexible enough to allow God to send him on a journey that would radically change his life. When you feel that all you have left is to rely upon God, get ready for the journey to take you anywhere the Master chooses.

■

Twenty years later, the church I pastor is based out of a hospital open twenty-four hours a day to serve some of the most broken people in Los Angeles. The vision is nothing like what I had when I came to this city. Honestly, I thought I would just come to church and people would naturally show up because I had it all together and that was it. The road didn't take me down that path.

God decided to give me—a pastor who is totally out of his league, out of his level of understanding, and a total work in progress—a four-hundred-thousand-square-foot hospital to help people. Another prayer I often pray is, "God, help me to stay teachable, never having it all figured out, but perfectly fine with the fact I don't understand the next step."

Now I pastor a church of misfits: girls who are victims of human trafficking, homeless families, people in rehab who have had lifelong drug addictions. It's a beautiful collection of people who are realizing day by day that God doesn't throw away leftover pieces. He redeems them. He collects them to reuse.

You are unique! Don't live in self-doubt. Realize that whatever you see as a flaw or a lack is an opportunity for God to use that beautiful place of vulnerability for His glory. We are all out of our element in some way. We are all in need of God's grace and His miracles.

Realizing you're a misfit means you understand you have more questions than answers. Maybe you feel out of place because of the way you were raised. Perhaps your parents pointed out your flaws. Or maybe in high school people noticed something about your personality that was different. Life simply has a way of breaking us down to the point where we feel our uniqueness is a curse to this world instead of a blessing.

Jesus loved working with rugged fishermen, prostitutes, and people whom nobody wanted. In fact, He loved misfits so much that He placed Rahab, a known prostitute, in His hall of heroes. David, whom He warmly called "a man after my own heart," also made the list (Acts 13:22). The same man who committed adultery and orchestrated a murder plot known as a man after God's own heart? This guy is in the ministry hall of fame? Yes, and it's an amazing picture of just how much God loves us.

He doesn't condone the mistakes in our lives, but often, when misfits realize that they need God for everything in their lives, it's a glorious connection. A life so perfectly attached to God's heart. Do you feel incapable? Then go ahead and pray sincere prayers. Those are ones that say, "God, I need You to show up because You are so much bigger than me." Misfits tend to pray for things that require God to show up.

Let me tell you about some people God used. When my church finally started to grow, we were hitting an attendance level of around fifty people. The challenge is that more than forty of those fifty were people who came on our buses from Skid Row. Skid Row is a place where people line both sides of several streets in the Los Angeles business district, sleeping around bonfires, cardboard boxes, and tents. Sadly, women and children occupy these cold, dark streets. There are pockets of Skid Row where people line up against walls and practically inject needles until they die—hence the name *Skid Row*.

Many years ago, our church received its first donation of a brand-new bus. We were so excited. We took that bus down to Skid Row, and during the course of a few months forty homeless people began regularly meeting us for rides to church. Can you imagine looking out on Sunday morning and nearly every person in the church being homeless? I was a pastor who didn't understand anything about homelessness, and I had a congregation of homeless people who just came for the free food after every service. A misfit pastor and a misfit congregation. We were all out of place.

Shockingly, the people started to come to church and bring their friends. Since 80 percent of the people in our church were homeless, we didn't have many volunteers, so God gave us an idea for a position called "Street Deacons." (Don't judge. You have to work with what you have!) I appointed these guys as church staff to help me get as many people on the bus to come to church as possible. You should've seen the smiles on the faces of some of these men.

They couldn't believe someone would love them, believe in them, and give them such a great title. One man cried when I told him that he could be a Street Deacon. Several of the men stopped drinking because they were so honored that they would have this chance. Many of the guys sobered up, dressed up, cleaned up because a pastor had given them a chance to have a role in the church. They went out on the streets and gathered up friends. Every week they would check in with me and give updates on their progress.

They lived for this chance and they made the best of it. They just needed someone to believe the best in them. The first staff members who joined me were an interesting collection of individuals. However, they were the seeds that would later grow into the miracle we now call the Dream Center.

We are often put in places where we know we are called to do something but really don't know how it's going to be done. Give God your limitations, tell Him about the ways you feel unqualified, and then give Him whatever you have left even if it feels like it's just a big bag of burdens. It's all God has ever wanted. That's why the Bible says in 1 Peter 5:7, "Cast all your anxiety on him because he cares for you."

God loves uniqueness. He loves you. Upon this foundation, we continue by saying, "Welcome, misfits." God's been waiting to use you.

two

MISFIT IDEAS

I will never forget a day that changed my life. It was the day of my nineteen-year anniversary of pastoring the Dream Center. A few weeks before the anniversary, in prayer, I felt impressed to do something that would shake up the church.

One of my greatest fears for Christian people is that we will start valuing safety over danger. God never called the church to be safe but to be dangerous. It's like something in football called the "prevent defense." The prevent defense is a strategy that says, "Don't try not to make a mistake; just try to survive the rest of the game. Sit in your protective shell and hope to ride out the clock."

When I watch football it seems that the prevent defense never works—same with life. The prevent lifestyle gives way too much attention to the possibility of failure. The entire book of Acts was about a dangerous mission and living on the edge. It was about people who took a risk for God and who succeeded, but sometimes failed. I rebel against any form of faith that says, "Just try to survive." I rebel against any level of a Christian walk that must play it safe.

One day I had an idea that grew into something we call Serve 24. The idea was for the church to do a twenty-four-hour nonstop outreach throughout the entire city of Los Angeles. We would invade the city all hours of the day, doing nothing but serving and extending radical grace. No sleep; no break. The people could choose an hour to serve, maybe two, and—if they were really hard core—they could serve all twenty-four.

We kicked off the outreach by giving away hot dogs from our hot dog cart on Skid Row. After passing out nearly a thousand hot dogs, we went to Long Beach to put on a children's church service and clothing store for the kids and parents. We delivered hygiene kits and blankets to the people on Venice Beach. Two hours later, we raced over to Hollywood Boulevard and listened to teens share their stories of running away from home and of the horrors of sexual abuse they endured as kids. These were teenage kids fighting to survive in a city that swallows up victims.

The city of Los Angeles looks much different after midnight than in the glittering daytime. At night the City of Angels becomes the city of broken hearts—full of people trying to fit in, runaways who believed they could make it in Hollywood only to find their fates trapped by a city that destroys more dreams than it builds.

It was tough going. As the clock ticked, I started to feel I couldn't handle much more. We learn a lot about our faith when we have to battle fatigue and the flesh that demands to have its way. I wanted the outreach to end, but we were only on hour fourteen. Ten hours left to overcome the flesh and to overcome the tears flowing nonstop from my eyes.

We have a home for girls who are victims of human trafficking at the Dream Center, and our staff wanted to show me the "track" the girls take in the middle of the night. It's the route the prostitutes are forced to work every single night. Driving through the streets at night and seeing girls everywhere forced to sell their bodies, I was shocked by how young they were. I couldn't make out the ages of the girls, but they were each somebody's daughter. Not long ago they were probably just doing the things children do.

Our team drove me down the street, and I saw the power of love. Our ladies who run our trafficking ministry, Project Hope, boldly approached these young ladies and asked, "Would you like a free gift?" Sitting in the backseat, I thought, *These girls are probably going to tell us to go away or be too embarrassed to take the gift.* Wrong. The girls were so overwhelmed somebody wanted to give them something that they literally jumped up and down. Some of them cried. It was the most moving experience to see those girls get that flower, the free lip gloss, the food, and just beam that somebody cared.

It was such a simple idea. Never did I realize that driving down a road, handing out flowers and lip gloss to prostitutes could mean so much. It was a simple idea. Some of the greatest ways we choose to serve are often the ones that do not make sense. Whenever those girls looked at that lip gloss, they saw a rescue number printed on the tube, and a reminder that someone cares.

■

Misfit ideas are often off-the-wall. When an idea comes to your mind and it has something to do with simple acts of service, here's my advice: *do it!* Don't overanalyze kindness. When an idea comes to your mind that has something to do with helping others, that means it is an idea from God.

I almost talked myself out of Serve 24 because it sounded crazy. Now I'm glad I didn't because it transformed so many people inside and outside our church. We actually started several different long-term outreach ministries because of it.

Misfit ideas require faith, and that might scare a lot of people who want God to work within their perfect, well-scripted boxes. The beginnings of great ideas and transformational concepts usually come in short bursts of inspiration. A safety mechanism within the human mind will often try to force them away to protect itself from taking a dramatic course in life. The secret is to let that crazy idea run wild in your mind for a while, to the point where you start visualizing great possibilities. You start seeing the people who could be helped from your willingness to think outside of your comfort and ease.

Misfit ideas are all over the Bible. Just take, for example, these incredible verses and the ideas that didn't make sense.

The masses were flocking to hear Jesus speak. Well out of town, they had no place to get food. The disciples came to Jesus and suggested He send them back to the villages to get food for themselves. They were thinking logically. Nothing wrong with that. "Send them home. It's not our responsibility to feed them. They can buy their own food."

But Jesus had an idea. "They do not need to go away," He said. "You give them something to eat" (Matt. 14:16). Often an unconventional idea is one that comes in the middle of a predictable problem. It's easy to say a problem is too hard to solve. It takes a hopeful idea to see the potential within the problem.

The disciples objected. "We have here only five loaves of bread and two fish," they said (v. 17).

Conventional thinking sees the facts. Faith calculates the formula of possibility.

"Bring them here to me," Jesus said (v. 18), and then started putting together a plan that made no earthly sense. Here's how the gospel describes what happened next:

> And he directed the people to sit down on the grass. Taking the five loaves and the two fish and looking up to heaven, he gave thanks and broke the loaves. Then he gave them to the disciples, and the disciples gave them to the people. (v. 19)

Jesus gave thanks for the miracle that was about to happen. He showed us that giving thanks before something happens is the gateway of faith. And what happened as a result? "They all ate and were satisfied, and the disciples picked up twelve basketfuls of broken pieces that were left over. The number of those who ate was about five thousand men, besides women and children" (vv. 20–21).

That's what an idea can mean. I think one of the important takeaways for us is that the miracle happened at the point of obedience. It sounded crazy, but the disciples listened to Jesus and did what He said anyway. The miracle was already on its way.

I wonder how many dreams have never been fulfilled because they didn't fit into our logic. We couldn't control the outcome so instead we tried to ignore it. Most ideas that make a difference are outside our comfort zones—whether it's a child starting a lemonade stand to raise money for an overseas cause, or a pastor trying to build a church, or a business owner wanting to prosper for a great purpose.

The unknown scares us, but God's ideas don't fit into the mold—and that's what makes them so incredible. The next time you say no to something because it doesn't make sense, ask yourself, *What could go right if I do say yes?*

Sometimes going to the next level only requires a change of perspective. Learning to embrace ideas that seem crazy will never be easy because it seems to endanger our safety, survival, and our predictable world. Everything that has ever happened at the Dream Center doesn't make sense on paper. But if it did make sense on paper it probably never would have worked.

In our human strength we are simply not good enough to execute a plan we think is perfect. In God's strength, even when stretched, there are no limitations.

■

It was the day before Thanksgiving. I was walking along a shopping center just enjoying the little holiday break. It was a beautiful day, which is usual for Los Angeles. Walking by a movie theater, I saw a poster for a movie I had wanted to see with my children, Disney's *Frozen*. But as I looked at the movie poster, a crazy idea came to me. *Take all the families who live at the Dream Center to see the movie.*

I calculated the expense in my head—as we all normally do—and almost talked myself out of doing it. This was far too expensive. There were thirty families who lived at the Dream Center. And have you seen the price of movie tickets in LA? They're not cheaper closer to the source. This would cost a couple thousand dollars when it was all said and done.

Then I started to nickel-and-dime the idea. Maybe I could cut out seeing it in 3D—that would save a lot of money. The excuses were piling up. It's called the talking-yourself-out phase of the idea.

I've noticed the wrestling match in my spirit before. It's the heavy wave of doubt that usually comes right before something special is about to happen. Faith has to overcome something in order to be faith. Practically, that means instead of caving in to doubt, we should see doubt as a verification that we are on the right track.

The answer was obvious: Listen to this prompting in my spirit and buy tickets for all the families and take them to the movies. It was rather humorous asking for a pile of tickets for a 10:30 a.m. movie. The manager even had to come out to make sure I was serious. I was, and he sold me the tickets. Mission accomplished, at least the first part. Then came the fun part. We phoned the Dream Center and told everyone to load up the buses. "We're leaving the facility tomorrow and going to the movies."

Walking up to the theater, I was greeted by the loving children who live on one of the floors of the Dream Center building, sprinting to embrace me in a way so special that it raced straight to my heart. We put our 3D glasses on and went into the theater. For some it was the first time they'd ever been in a theater. Hearing them say so was enough to melt my heart.

Then, like a beautiful angel, a little girl named Ava sat next to me. I'm guessing she was five years old. She was the kind of girl whose toothless smile was so big, bold, and beautiful that you wanted to take her home. She sat right next to me. Kids' popcorn and candy in hand, she reclined in her seat, munching away. I met a friend—a very special one.

Ava didn't know what to do with the 3D glasses. She kept taking them on and off, wondering what the picture was like with the naked eye. Honestly, it was driving me crazy. I wanted her to enjoy the movie with the full experience in 3D. When you love someone, you want them to see life through the perfect lens.

When the movie was over, once again she embraced me with gratitude, big smiles, and a warm heart. I thought, *What a wonderful experience.*

But there's more to the story.

I later found out Ava's mother was a lady who graduated our home for victims of human trafficking. Her mother was trafficked across state lines and eventually settled at the Dream Center. This sweet little girl, Ava, who won my heart, was born from a pimp who was controlling nearly every part of Ava's mom's life. Her mother had made extraordinary steps to get free from "the game," as they call it in prostitution and trafficking.

A few days after the movie, I was taking a man on a tour of our facility. We arrived at a floor where the families were about to greet us and tell their amazing stories of changing from homelessness to the hope they have found at the Dream Center. Ava saw me, ran, and jumped into my arms. She hugged me stronger than a lineman hugging his quarterback after a touchdown. I never knew fifty pounds could feel so powerful.

Then I realized that one movie, one moment of going out of my convenience-loving thought process, was a moment I would make a very special friend. That hug was worth more than the twelve hundred dollars spent that day.

Sure, the idea was sudden, but that's what made it so powerful. Talking yourself out of compassion usually leads to regret—or to a life that continues inward to the point where everything becomes absorbed in feeding your growing "Me" monster.

I used to always try to talk myself out of spontaneous ideas. Now I surrender to them. I've realized I'm not a good enough person to think of a sudden compassionate idea on the spot. That's not me. The sudden idea of irresistible compassion that floods my soul is from God. Every day, in big ways and small ways, I'm trying to see that willingness to trust and be led has an ending that will glorify God.

New ideas can't be regulated to a planning board. You can't always calculate compassion. The best plans are often the ones we have to navigate through one blind moment of obedience at a time. Misfit ideas are just that. They don't add up. They wage war against the comfort of a life flowing in a direction we can control.

The world needs abnormal thinkers. There are no perfect plans—just compassionate ones. If the idea doesn't make sense, there's a good chance it might make history. Have there been times in your life when you were compelled to act, to make a difference? Times in your life when everything inside you said, *Jump! Go for it.*

The worst that can happen is you could fail to make a difference. But I have a pretty good feeling you will succeed when you seek to bring joy to someone else's world. You might just get a hug that's worth more than money, and you just might meet a friend like Ava who will change your life.

Misfit thinkers always seem to live life aggressively rather than passively. They choose to live life and not let life live them. They are the kind of people who will drive home a different way just to see life from a different perspective; the kind of people who will see the meaning behind the mundane; the kind of people who strategize ways they can make a difference before they even arrive where they are going; the kind of people who decide the attitude they will have before they even get to the place where they are going.

They are addicted to life—addicted to making a difference.

My father has been in the ministry for sixty years. I remember the days of great notoriety, when *Time* magazine listed his church as one of the largest in America. He was one of the first to ever build a building that would hold nearly sixty-five hundred seats. Every year, I see in him the man I want to become.

Yes, he was one of the first guys ever to pastor a megachurch of ten thousand in Phoenix, Arizona. Yes, Tommy Barnett is a household ministry name. At seventy-six years of age, he's not just going strong; he's raging against the common, institutional way of boring ministry.

I've been impressed by his ability to build a big church, but not half so much as I'm impressed with the way he really lives ministry. The man gets up every morning and unleashes upon this world his life full of hope-filled pursuits. My father is the ultimate misfit thinker. I never saw my father as a megachurch builder, but as a man with a megacause.

My entire life of ministering to the homeless and forgotten is because of his example. Every Sunday he would bring the homeless to his church building. He spent thousands of dollars buying buses for people who could give him nothing in return. In fact, he lost many church members because they didn't want to bring their families to a church that attracted "those kinds of people."

But he stayed the course, never wavered. He never let the super-clean, overly religious crowd steal his love for the hurting. He brought the homeless to church, even gave them haircuts, and did it at the expense of losing people.

Conventional thinking would say, *Protect your success. Know your market. Build a society that Christians would feel safe to visit.*

My father never believed the church was called to be safe, but rather that it was called to be on the edge. He would say things like, "If you're not living on the edge, you're taking up too much space." One of his favorite lines is, "I am a need hunter." That means he spends his life looking for ways to meet needs.

Even in the midst of building one of the first great megachurches, he still went to the housing projects, picked people up, and brought them to church in his own car. It's those moments that make you believe in ministry, and in the good of people—people who don't only *know* what is right, but also *do* what is right.

My father is a man who believes quite simply that if something is right, then you should do it. Figure out a way later. The ideas of a compassionate, spontaneous man like him might seem so idealistic that some would even label them irresponsible or childish. People who love Christ, however, don't care about labels, but rather about the cause. And the only cause that matters is the cause of Christ.

God has called you to make a difference. The difference might not be buying a hospital or housing the homeless. Need is everywhere. You have a sphere of influence that makes you special and unique. Maybe your misfit idea is helping a child pay for a field trip his parents can't afford, or it could mean emptying your closet to rush clothes down to a shelter. Whatever it is, here's the point: If it's spontaneous, full of love, and will make a difference, then move in faith. And don't waste time.

■

I love the story of when Jesus encountered the crippled man by the pool of Bethesda. There were many others like him there. The sick and disabled would wait waterside, because word on the street was that an angel would sometimes come down and stir up the pool. When that happened, the first person in the water would be healed. Of course if you were disabled, you could hardly sprint down to the water, and this guy had been waiting for thirty-eight years.

"Do you want to get well?" Jesus asked him.

"Sir," he answered, "I have no one to help me into the pool when the water is stirred. While I am trying to get in, someone else goes down ahead of me."

There was no need for that race any longer. "Get up!" said Jesus. "Pick up your mat and walk." And just like that the man was instantly healed (John 5:6–8).

In the gospel story, it quickly adds that Jesus healed this man on the Sabbath. That means Jesus healed on a day considered off-limits by the religious. Curing this man was a forbidden concept. It didn't fit the order of the way things should go. Everything about this story is off the radar of normal reasoning. Not only did Jesus heal on the Sabbath, but this man had been crippled for thirty-eight years—13,870 days! His hopes had been dashed for so long that he had simply given up.

Then Jesus came along and threw everything into a tailspin. He had compassion on the man but, at the same time, wanted him to shoulder his responsibilities. Jesus said, "Get up! Pick up your mat and walk." The man must have been shocked that Jesus was asking him to do something he could not do. The truth is, God doesn't always ask us to do what we can do, but rather to do more than we can do. He told this man to do something he was totally incapable of doing, but it turned out well for the man!

Jesus didn't speak to this man's need but spoke to his potential. Meanwhile, the man could have considered Jesus' request to be some kind of sick joke. But he moved, and he got his miracle.

■

Go ahead and move. Take the steps God is calling you to take. The ideas might be out of touch with what others might consider reality. It's okay. Misfit ideas are not supposed to make sense to everyone else. They are perfectly unique to your gifts, your talents, your inspiration. It's perfectly fine to have misfit ideas. The Bible makes it clear in Romans 12:2, "Do not conform to the pattern of this world, but be transformed by the renewing of your mind."

It certainly sounds to me as if there's a special reward for divergent thinking. In your life, what have you always wanted to do and talked yourself out of? Move in the direction of the extraordinary idea and watch Jesus come along and make it happen. Just start moving.

three

LOOKING FOR MISFITS

Every once in a while, a new student will come into my kids' class at school. As soon as my kids are in the car, they are always quick to tell me when a new student arrives. They tell me all about the person, where they are from, and that it was their first day in school. Early on in life, I want them to learn to look for people who feel out of place—to look for the misfits. The first thing I tell them is, "Go and make them feel welcome. Whatever it takes, go out of your way to let them know they are special."

The world is more connected than ever before and, yet, more lonely. The mark of a Bible-believing Christian is someone who looks for people who feel misplaced in the world.

Jesus looked for what we would call "the fish out of water." In one story He came to the city of Jericho—the same city Joshua conquered generations before. There was a man there named Zacchaeus who really wanted to see who Jesus was; he'd heard the rumors but he wanted to see for himself.

But there was a problem. Zacchaeus was short—"a wee little man" as the children's song goes—and there was a massive crowd around Jesus. What could he do? He spotted a tree and climbed up to get a better view. It wasn't long before Jesus saw him.

"Zacchaeus," He said, "come down immediately. I must stay at your house today" (Luke 19:5). Let's stop right there for a moment. *I must stay at your house today.* Isn't it great that Jesus invited Himself over to this man's house? Jesus pushed Himself into Zacchaeus's life.

I still don't know how Zacchaeus was able to stay in that tree from the shock factor of Jesus noticing him among the crowd celebrating His entrance into the city. On top of that, Jesus invited Himself over. What a savior! He takes notice even of the ones who feel forsaken and hidden among the shadows.

The Bible says Zacchaeus came down from his limb and welcomed Jesus, but that people started talking smack. "He has gone to be the guest of a sinner," they said (Luke 19:7). You see, Zacchaeus was a tax collector—the chief tax collector—and there was no one in Israel more despised than a tax collector.

But the people got this all wrong. Jesus wasn't invited to be the guest of a sinner; He invited Himself to be with the sinner. The entire life of Jesus from the womb to the resurrection was about one thing: *looking for misfits.* Jesus didn't wait for misfits to find Him; He went after them with incredible intensity and awareness.

There's another similar passage of Scripture that might escape you unless you're really paying attention. It's found in Matthew 26:6: "While Jesus was in Bethany in the home of Simon the Leper . . ." Now, I realize this Scripture didn't immediately blow your mind. On the surface it isn't particularly powerful—but get the context. Jesus was near the end of His ministry. He was in the final stage of His life before going through the agony of the cross.

What would I be doing in the final stages of my life, near the end? Probably saying good-bye to family, or maybe doing something fun, or taking a dream vacation, possibly eating at a really good steak house somewhere.

Jesus? He was having dinner at the home of a man who was infected with the social-outcast disease of leprosy. This pretty much explains the life of Jesus. Looking for anyone who felt invisible or forsaken and going out of His way to find them. The entire plan of salvation is Jesus leaving heaven to come down to earth to find the outsiders in their sins, and then to save them from their sins.

Jesus' encounters with out-of-place people were transformational. People were changed after being around Him. Jesus had a way of noticing them and then believing they could be so much more. As a result, people were changed. Jesus surrounded Himself with some pretty bizarre characters. He sought them out. Then they flocked to Him and became the people who would start a revolution.

Here's the thing: looking for misfits is our job too.

■

Every day I go to the office at the Dream Center, it's a life-changing experience. I usually run into a couple of dozen people from our recovery program cleaning up the parking lot or doing chores near my office. They usually have smiles on their faces, and some even pray as they work. They humble this pastor with their raw devotion.

Here I am strolling into the office at 8:30 a.m. and people in the recovery program have been up since 5:30 a.m. praying and studying the Bible. It's as if they have conquered the world before daybreak. Many of these dedicated people may one day serve on the church's staff. In fact, 70 percent of our staff graduated from our recovery program. We're talking about former meth addicts, heroin users, and prostitutes. At our church we have ex drug addicts, pimps, and murderers—and that's just the pastoral staff. You know you've got an outreach church when your ushers wear ankle bracelet monitors.

Never before in my life did I realize God could do so much with such raw material, the kinds of people in the early parts of my ministry who I thought were too far gone to change. How can those people ever turn the corner? They are damaged goods. Now they are my church staff, and more are coming down the pipeline of our Savior's misfit production line.

I used to look at people with lifelong drug addictions and think, *Maybe I can help them survive.* Now I look at them and say, "One day they are going to thrive." I've learned that being loved and believed in are the only things most people need to turn the corner.

Have you ever noticed that the church has some of the strangest people? As a pastor of an outreach church, I've seen it all. I've seen people come to church on our buses dressed up like Bible characters. Some were even self-proclaimed disciples. I've seen a man bring an actual finger puppet to church to join him while he praised God. One lady—no kidding—used to bring a frozen chicken and make dance moves with its arms in church during worship.

Then, of course, at the Dream Center we have dancing. Lloyd is a man in his seventies who will do a hip-hop dance whenever called upon. Lloyd has been coming since the church started and is now considered the Dream Center mascot.

Your church doesn't have to be an outreach church in a major urban center to have a few eccentrics. Why do people like that feel so connected to the church? The reason the church has so many diverse people is that we are the only place that will welcome them.

If you go to a nightclub, you won't see those people being let in the doors. They would never make it past the bouncers. Restaurants will often kick out someone with bizarre behavior. Hotels? You've got to have the money to stay there, so that disqualifies many people. The church has the greatest collection of colorful people because deep in these people's hearts they know that Jesus is for everyone.

The church's strength is not how many perfect people we have, or wealthy, or cool. The church is for the outcast as well, the misfit. A church that tries to create an environment by eliminating this element is practicing the religious version of "selective breeding."

Can people be difficult, demanding, even annoying? Sure. But the number of colorful, interesting, challenging personalities in your church is its best measure of strength. If you've got none, you need to open up the invitation. The world is our demographic. Everyone is our mission! We must welcome the people overlooked the most.

My message here is simple: embrace people who might act or look different. There's no other place that will accept them but the church. I think that's a great compliment. The church is not a waiting room for the saints but a hospital room for the sick. The world is not fighting to flood their establishments with this clientele. I sure hope we do!

And don't think this applies only to the church. It applies to everyone. Do we really go out of our way to help the abandoned? Are we more inconvenienced by the actions of misfits than the opportunity to lend a hand? When there's an accident on the freeway, are we more concerned with the ten-minute delay and the extra time we have to spend in traffic, or are we truly concerned about the condition of the people in the wreck? Don't even mention stopping and helping! The battle rages on within us. Do we extend a hand or play it safe? I wonder how many times I've played it safe when I could have gone the extra mile.

Life is so much better when we live it looking for ways to be a blessing. My father always used to tell me, "You live life palms up, you will only be happy at Christmas time and your birthday. You live life with palms down, you can be happy 365 days a year." For him, a palms-down life involved looking for people who feel invisible in this world. After all, that's what Jesus did.

This is the great secret to joy: "Find a need and fill it, find a hurt and heal it."* I almost lost sight of that even as a pastor. In fact, I considered giving up in ministry. I became lost in my own self-pity, my own discouragement, until one day God dropped a revelation from heaven that changed my life. He encouraged me to start seeking out misfits.

After years in LA, the ministry had become self-sustaining. I had a great staff in place that could do the one-on-one ministry. I convinced myself that I had a right to manage the miracle rather than personally touch and feel the hurts of our city. Eighteen years of ministry, thousands of lives fed, housed, you have a right to raise up leaders to do that. Right? But God spoke to me to throw myself back into the trenches and serve with a renewed heart. Maybe some of you can relate. Following is my story in more detail.

■

Have you ever had the feeling you were living on some kind of Christian autopilot? Have you had a time in your life when nothing moves you and you have no idea how you are going to

---

* Robert Schuller: http://www.cbn.com/700club/Guests/Interviews/Robert _Schuller050505.aspx.

get free? It's as if your mind is moving, but your heart is frozen. Have you ever been stuck in that place not just for a day, not just for a week, but for a whole season of your life? You want to feel again, but your heart becomes a stubborn wall that just won't cave in.

I had never felt that way in my life until year eighteen in ministry. "Why do I feel this way, God?" I prayed. "I'm only a thirty-eight-year-old pastor and life has been wonderful." Right up to that point, that is.

I started to feel the agonizing process of getting mad at myself because I wasn't content. I knew I had so much going for me that I became irritated at myself for not seeing it. It's a cycle of sadness and condemnation, and the carousel continues. For me the stage lasted several months. Can anyone else identify with this?

But then everything changed. Never will I forget that night. It was a Thursday night church service. Before every offering I have someone from our recovery program give a testimony on how their life has changed since living at the Dream Center. It's the highlight of the service. Usually it's someone who has had a lifetime of drug problems and has now been clean for months. They share their story, and the crowd goes wild.

This particular night a man gave a testimony on how he and his son were living on the cold streets of Skid Row, homeless. One night a Dream Center bus picked them up and brought them to church. The father was days away from losing his kids to foster care, but because the Dream Center gave him a place to live his life was restored. At the end of his testimony he fell to his knees, looked up at me, and said, "Pastor, thank you for saving my life."

I immediately felt the Holy Spirit prompt me to fall to my knees and get lower than the man and tell him how much of an honor it was to serve him. I fell to my knees at a position lower than his already humble posture and said, "Thank you for allowing me to serve you." Then the phrase *"You get to serve"* flooded my heart. It was the Spirit talking.

The revelation was beautiful, but God wasn't done. The next day, I got a phone call from the elementary school down the street that we as the church had adopted. We put thousands of dollars into that elementary school because it had so much need. Funding had been cut in the Los Angeles school districts, so we as a church decided we would fill the gap.

We decided to give weekly grocery bags from our mobile food truck to every parent at the school who needed it. We also provide toys for every student at Christmas and have raised thousands of dollars for new technology for the classrooms. It has become a beautiful partnership between the church and the public school.

I picked up the phone to answer a call from the school. "Pastor, the kids have written a song to say thank you for helping the school," said the principal of Rosemont Elementary. "They love the Dream Center and want to dedicate this song. They wrote the lyrics and the melody. You've got to come hear it."

Honestly, I didn't want to go. I really didn't want to do

anything. Discouragement affects us that way. It paralyzes us from even embracing good things. But I realized I couldn't let the children down, so I made my way down the street to this underfunded urban school.

On the way, a homeless man with a shopping cart said, "Hey, Pastor, I just got a meal at the Dream Center. Thank you!" His toothless smile was so big it verged on adorable. I gave him a high five, and then those words once again invaded my spirit. *You get to serve that homeless man.* Twice this phrase had blasted in my spirit as if through a megaphone.

I continued down the road, entered the school, and walked into the assembly where these precious children were preparing to sing their thank-you song. I didn't realize how big a deal this was. It appeared as though the children had been preparing for weeks to present this song, and the teachers had brought every type of food for my staff and me. Mexican food, Asian food, Filipino food—they spread out an international buffet. And let's face it, when free food is involved the day always gets brighter.

The children at Rosemont Elementary took the stage and began to put on quite a production. The wide variety of ethnicity on that stage was like a beautiful rainbow. I was expecting to hear one song, but I got a concert. They were showing off their hip-hop moves, patriotic songs, and a beautiful diversity of songs from every ethnicity. I looked at those kids on stage and I noticed the clothes many of them were wearing. I'd seen them at the Dream Center clothing store. The church was the resource center for every part of many of these kids' lives.

Then a teacher announced the song they would sing honoring the Dream Center. Here are a few lines of the song so beautifully crafted by the children of Rosemont.

> *Who would of believed that this song was in me,*
> *the song was in me?*
> *Who would of seen that it would set me free,*
> *set me free?*
> *All I needed was a chance, one opportunity,*
> *a person just like you who saw the very best in me.*

For the first time in a long while, I was starting to feel again. I walked out of that assembly cherishing the words of that song, especially these: "All I needed was a chance, one opportunity, a person just like you who saw the very best in me." But the words that thundered in my spirit? *You get to serve those kids.*

This was it! This was the revelation I needed to get me off autopilot. I was living my life with a "have-to-serve" mind-set rather than a "get-to-serve." Just like that, the fire flickered and burned again. No longer would I see the calling of my life as obligation, but opportunity. From that day on, that revelation has been driven into my heart and into the heart of our church.

When we live our lives under the weight of "have-to-serve," at some point we won't want to. But when we live our lives with a "get-to-serve" mind-set, we will want more. The get-to-serve life looks for ways to be a blessing, doesn't mind inconvenience, and serves out of pure joy. The Bible says this about Jesus: "For the joy set before him he endured the cross, scorning its shame, and sat down at the right hand of the throne of God" (Heb. 12:2).

Underline "For the joy set before him." Jesus gave His life for the joy of saving mankind, the joy of redemption, the joy of suffering for our freedom. He did all of the above for the joy of giving us a future.

Never let anyone try to condemn you into serving or belittle you for not loving more. Serving is joy! Any other motivation other than that will fade away. When I was living under the have-to-serve frame of mind, it almost crushed my future. I almost quit the ministry. Guilt is not a proper motivation to unleash a servant's heart.

The get-to-serve attitude and revelation from God saved my life. Unleash your gifts upon this world; look for opportunities to find the misfit, the marginalized, the forgotten; and bless people's socks off. Or in some cases, get them some socks to put on.

■

Have you been looking for ways to bless people lately? You don't have to look far. Just look anywhere, wherever you happen to be.

One day some of our leaders noticed that our young girls around the neighborhood were growing up and becoming ladies. It was normal in that neighborhood for girls thirteen years of age to give away their virginity. Prostitution is rampant in various parts of Los Angeles. With lack of value placed on their lives, they become vulnerable to a life of prostitution. We wanted to reach these girls before the pimps did. We wanted to reinforce the idea that they are beautiful, valuable, and called by God to remain pure. We needed to take action or the predators would.

As a result, we brought twenty-five teen girls to the Dream Center chapel for a purity night. The room was beautifully decorated like a Grammy party. The scene was breathtaking. So much effort was put into that party that the old Dream Center gym looked like a scene out of *Cinderella*. The girls arrived with curled hair, wearing dresses and heels. Men in the Dream Center Leadership School escorted them into their palace for the night. The men served the girls their meals and refreshments, showing the girls how they deserved to be treated.

The queen of the night, my wife, Caroline Barnett, then delivered a sermon on purity. I've seen a lot of churches preach on purity to youth groups in Middle America, but for some reason in the heart of this city it seemed to have an extra-special meaning. The event ended with the girls receiving purity rings and prayer from their leaders.

Today many of the girls are part of our Youth Leadership program at the Dream Center. They know they are loved and valued and someone is looking out for them and willing to fight for their future. A miracle happened that night, all because some people had the idea to look for the vulnerable and create a moment that would change their lives.

People are in need, and whatever you have to give is enough when it's given from the motivation of "get-to-serve."

Some will say, "When I get a building one day, then I'll help hurting people, or maybe when my money ship comes in." There's no ideal place to start serving. It's not a destination; it's a daily journey. We serve now with whatever we have.

Maybe all you have is pain in your life; so serve out of pain. Maybe you only have a few pennies to spare; so spare them. Maybe you've got a big smile; so let it loose. There are too many people who feel unloved who need whatever you have left to give. Go looking and start giving. Trust me—it's enough when it's given from the abundance of love.

four

EMBRACING MISFITS

Let me tell you about a husband and wife whom I admire greatly: Jeannie and Charlie Johnston. They moved from Phoenix into the same apartment complex my wife and I lived in.

One day I went to the garage of the apartment complex and saw a truck that was loaded up with an extraordinary amount of food. It wasn't just your average big-family Costco run; it was food fit for the masses. And not only food—they also had a hot dog cart with them.

"Where are you going?" I asked.

"We are going to look for homeless people to feed," they said. "We just moved here."

Jeannie and Charlie and their three children had just moved to Los Angeles, and their first concern was feeding the homeless. I told them I was the pastor of a place called the Dream Center. "I've got a pretty good idea of where to find the people who need food the most," I said. Instantly we had a connection.

Jeannie and Charlie—who now is known as Hot Dog Charlie—changed our lives. They are a perfect example of how one person can make a difference if they follow through with their dreams. Every Tuesday, the Johnstons took money out of their own pockets and loaded up their hot dog cart. Their home church, New Life Arizona, had helped them buy the hot dog cart and also helped get them started. Not only that, but their church was helping to finance the supplies and operating costs every week. It caught like wildfire. Their friends donated money, their family donated money, and even random people driving by the cart gave them money because they were so inspired.

They had a sign that said, "Free hot dogs and free prayer." Through the prayers and support of this team of believers, they made the impossible come true and fed thousands in just a short amount of time. The Johnstons lived to give, and because they had the guts to take a chance on a crazy idea, they found their calling. The hot dog cart was their life, it was their mission, and it was their family legacy. It still is.

The hot dog cart not only fed a lot of people but, teamed up with the Dream Center, it also got a lot of people off the street. People would eat a hot dog, get prayer, and choose to go into one of our recovery programs. The partnership was perfect, and many lives have been changed.

The Johnstons and Hot Dog Charlie moved back to Arizona but I promise you, he's loading up a truck somewhere on a Tuesday doing what he always does: serving people. Here is a family that truly understands the joy of living for others. It's one thing to look for misfits, as discussed earlier, but embracing misfits leads to action. This family was on a mission, and they have found their lifelong cause.

The Dream Center has a hot dog cart of its own now, one that Charlie donated to us. We have bought our second truck, and a third is on the way, all because of an ordinary, hardworking family that decided to show us the power of simple love. One day hot dog carts will be all over the city of Los Angeles because of a family who took a simple idea and used it to help others. We get calls weekly about the cart; the idea is going global.

Looking back at Hot Dog Charlie and Jeannie, I realize it wasn't really their creative idea that was so special. It was their core belief that everyone was created in the image of God and everyone should be treated with dignity. Love was the driving force behind everything.

■

The world has a pretty good idea about what the church is against, but sometimes I wonder if they know what we are for. Have we become known as the people who are against everything? I certainly hope not.

Do we have an agenda that is clear in our love for the forsaken? The truth is, the way we treat others in this world is a sermon in itself. Wouldn't it be great if Christians in every area of influence were simply known as people going about doing good?

People might not understand everything about our relationship with God, but they see the way we treat people and our faith is expressed in a way they can understand. We do good things because we are empowered by a great God. When we comfort the afflicted, we start living like Jesus and we start changing the atmosphere of places everywhere we go.

Every believer ought to pursue a habit of loving people, embracing people. When we do, it becomes contagious. The great thing about being there for people who are misfits is the way we build confidence in them to dream again. Many people who feel life is over feel that way because they can't see through the walls of mistakes. They need someone to fight for them so that they can rise again, dream again.

When people come to the Dream Center to check in, it's usually in total desperation. Many are living on the streets, out of their cars—the new mobile shantytown shacks of America. Usually embarrassed, they come to the Dream Center wanting to find shelter.

The first question we ask them is, "What is your dream?"

The question takes them aback. "How can you ask me about my dream when I'm just trying to find a place to stay?"

We tell them not to worry about survival; that's all taken care of. Rest, eat, and let's talk about your dream.

Asking someone about his or her dream is a game changer. It immediately pulls people out of a place of survival and into the expectation of thinking about living. People want to be challenged; they want to be stretched, but they just don't know it's possible to even think that way. The families stabilize, they have a safe place to live, and then we embrace them by challenging them. Serving is not just about giving away stuff; it's about provoking one another toward good works. When we love someone, we don't want them to stay where they are; we want to challenge them to a better future.

Our family often takes long trips from Los Angeles to Phoenix to visit my family. Most trips we drive back at night to miss the morning traffic in Los Angeles. The conversation usually turns from chatty to super quiet around the ten o'clock hour. The kids have had enough and have fallen asleep. When we arrive home, I do what so many of you loving parents do: I hold them, pick them up, and take them into the house. I carry them to their rooms because I know there's a better place of rest there.

This is how God wants us to see people who are hurting in our world. Embrace them so we can carry them to a better place. The heads of the families who live at the Dream Center are getting their GED diplomas, going to college, or working. Love welcomes people but helps carry them to a better place. Reaching people means we want to carry them farther.

Jesus provides a powerful example of this. Early in the gospel of Matthew He called His first disciples to come and follow Him. These were rough guys, fishermen. "Follow me," said Jesus. "I will make you fishers of men" (Matt. 4:19 ESV). The Bible says they dropped their nets and came after Jesus.

Jesus invited these men out of their lives and challenged

them to live for something greater. He believed in them and wanted to take them on the adventure of a lifetime. He took these unqualified men and allowed them to first belong, in order that they might later believe.

■

Religion often says, "When you believe, then we will let you belong." But Jesus lived the concept that "when you belong, then you'll believe." Demanding belief first is not embracing misfits. It's conditional. *You must meet my conditions for perfection, and then I'll let you into my world.*

Belonging first says, *I'm not scared to help you in the middle of your mess and not afraid to take you along on the journey.* Jesus took these rough men on a journey full of love, correction, and power-packed moments. Jesus embraced these men and allowed them to belong to something far greater than they could ever imagine. Then He challenged them with a compelling mission.

Do you remember the Serve 24 outreach I mentioned earlier, when the church did nonstop outreach for twenty-four straight hours? I met a very special man on hour thirteen at Venice Beach. His name was Ray. We were just walking the boardwalk handing out hygiene products in the middle of the night when I came across this surprisingly joyful man who lived homeless on the beach.

I gave him a hygiene kit and socks (which are like gold in

ministering to the homeless). More than grateful, he was jubilant. He even did a little dance to say thank you. There's always a layer of gratitude when you help someone, but this man acted like he had won the lottery when he received his hygiene kit.

I was taken aback by this man's gratitude at something so simple. Ray was about six-foot-two and 175 pounds. He lived on the sand. He was an African American with dreadlocks and a joyful persona. After we gave him the goods, he made a strange request.

"Hey, dude, you want to play Frisbee?"

That sure came out of nowhere! It was two in the morning and this guy wanted to play Frisbee. I've experienced many things in outreach ministry, but this was certainly a first. But, why not? When in Venice Beach, do as the people in Venice Beach do (within the law and reason).

We started playing Frisbee on the sand in wild, wacky Venice Beach. The strangest collection of people make their residence on Venice Beach. There was a fog in the air, and it wasn't just the ocean fog. The smell of marijuana permanently floods the beach.

It didn't take long to learn that Ray was an expert at the game of Frisbee. He knew every style of Frisbee throw. He could float them up in the air or like a bullet throw the perfect line-drive Frisbee. He taught me techniques of Frisbee throwing, how to hold it, and how to make dramatic catches behind my back. Every time I would catch the Frisbee, Ray would brag on me. We had a blast. But wait a minute: I was supposed to be ministering to him, and here was Ray encouraging me. His gift back to me was his time and his Frisbee skills, and it certainly was a gift.

We talked about life, talked about living on the beach homeless, talked about it all. We didn't have a cup of coffee. We didn't go to a café. We just had some Frisbee fellowship. It was perfect. When we finished, Ray said, "Pastor, I want to give this to you." He wrote a nice message on the Frisbee, along with a smiley face, and gave me the specially autographed Frisbee. The kind gesture reminded me of the widow in the Bible who gave her last mite. Ray gave me his last Frisbee.

I think about that night often. I think about how compassion opens doors. Friendship usually precedes faith.

■

Embracing misfits is often risky. All good things are. Sure, people will walk over you. But if you want to be a bridge of hope, you have to be willing to be stepped on. Yes, people will take advantage of you. But compassion often throws caution to the wind, and that wind takes us to some pretty exciting places to serve.

Embracing misfits is also often misunderstood. There are times when it's not popular to help certain people because a family, or a community, or even a nation feels these people are not worthy of being loved. Embracing misfits means standing by people even when it's unpopular. The church ought to set world records on how fast we sprint to rescue the fallen. It's so easy to love someone at the top of their game, but it takes real character to love someone at the bottom.

I have a friend named Mike Foster. Mike Foster has a blog titled *People of the Second Chance*. When you have had a bad day, that's the place to go. The entire blog is about radical grace and running to people who are falling. He doesn't always take the popular stance regarding helping others, but it's always the right one. From following him on Twitter and other social media, I've learned that whenever someone falls, fails, or becomes an object of public scorn, here comes Mike armed with encouragement. He believes in the power of the second chance. He also believes that is the mark of a great Christian.

He doesn't really explain why he gives people second chances; he just does it. Everything about his life exudes second chances. He has learned that joy is not in further breaking something that is broken, but in putting the pieces back together. He sprints to the fallen because he realizes just how much Jesus did that for us. I visit his blog often, especially when I need to tip the scales of grace back into balance after I become contaminated with the flow of negativity and pessimism that so easily occupies our culture.

Generosity is a great way to live life. Generous people don't think about what they lose when they give; they think about what they've multiplied in someone else. Loving people unconditionally is sometimes difficult because they don't often get up as fast as we want them to, or even take advantage of the lifeline we give them. Don't get frustrated when someone you choose to embrace won't change. Just keep showing up in that person's life as a bridge of hope.

When someone is trying to make a comeback, offer your shoulders so that person can climb higher. Love people between the gaps of where they are and where they need to be. We never act more like Jesus than when we give someone a second chance. It's not the position of serving that makes the call of God so great; it's the privilege of serving. Going to bed at night knowing you believed the best in fallen humanity carries its own reward.

To some degree we are all unfit to serve, but let me give you a beautiful formula in God's kingdom. Here it is:

MESSED UP PEOPLE,

HELPING MESSED UP PEOPLE,

REALLY MESSES UP THE DEVIL

There are times when we should stand up for people when it's unpopular. Not because it's unpopular but because it pleases God. The heart to restore others moves the heart of God. This belief is really tested at times.

■

I want to share with you an experience that changed my life as a little boy. During my time playing Pop Warner football,

I witnessed more than one overzealous, yelling parent on the sidelines. I think we are all aware that parents can get out of control rooting for their kids from the stands. There's nothing that justifies a parent's bad behavior. It doesn't help the kids play better and it does not improve team spirit; there's just nothing good that comes from overbearing parents yelling from the sidelines.

One particular game, the team we were playing committed a penalty. The referee threw the yellow flag onto the field and called the violation. It's natural. It happens. It's football. Everyone expected it. But no one was expecting what was about to happen next.

The father of the boy who committed the penalty started to scream in total anger. He did not agree with the call, and he let the referee know about it. He ran onto the field and got in the ref's face. The referee was trying to calm the parent down, but he wouldn't stop. He was going to keep going until he proved his point. The official decided to throw another yellow flag at the parent for bad behavior.

What started as one penalty flag in favor of our team became a laundry room of flags. One after another, the referee penalized the other team for this father's behavior. When all was said and done, the angry father cost his son's team seventy-five yards in penalties.

Flags were not enough to stop this angry father who was no doubt embarrassing his son. It was a disaster on every level. The parents were angry that the man had lost his head, and eventually he was ejected from the premises. He held his head down in shame, realizing what he had just done, and was heading to the parking lot. All the parents were angry about this dad's behavior, and I don't blame them.

I looked into the stands to see how my father would react. My dad got up from the stands, walked out to the parking lot, and did the unpopular thing. He put his arm around the man and had a conversation with him. He sat with that man in his car and talked about his life's challenges. When my dad mentioned he was a pastor, the man was able to communicate all the struggles he had been facing.

At first I didn't get it. Why be nice to this man who had made a fool out of himself and embarrassed his kid? He didn't deserve my dad's kindness. Now, looking back, I get it. Even people who are wrong need a friend.

Embracing people who don't always make the right decisions and walking them back to health is one of the most incredible ways to live life. I'm not saying we justify people's actions. We love people in spite of their weaknesses, and we earn the right to coach them through better decisions in the future. Before we can coach someone back to life, they need to feel unconditional love. The man would later attend my dad's church simply because my father chose to encourage a man who was certainly the misfit of the hour.

Here's what I know: The masses are usually wrong in the way they treat people. It takes character to stand for restoration when it's so easy to kick someone while they are down.

The truth is, if we want to really help people make better decisions in their lives, we have to earn the right to be heard by first blasting them with unconditional love when they need it the most. Grace is the ability to see what someone can become even though they've counted themselves out.

The church is not a social club of fake perfection. It's a place where broken people fall in love with a perfect God. People who have learned the power of restoration have learned to love people where they are, not where they're supposed to be.

Don't you love people who see your potential more than your flaws? Gus Gabriel was like that. He was one of the church pillars remaining in the church I started to pastor at age twenty. A young, white, suburban pastor in the inner city equals totally unqualified.

The church only had a couple of dozen members, but they were going through a transition from an eighty-year-old pastor to a twenty-year-old pastor. The church really didn't see much potential in me. Truthfully, I didn't see much potential in myself. People in the church wanted another pastor who was more experienced, mature, and ready.

Gus was the spokesman for the church, and he took some bullets for this young leader. He loved me, never said one negative word to me, and stood behind me because he saw something in me that I didn't see in myself. He knew I would have to go through layers of new things while transitioning to this new life, and he decided he was going to be with me one layer at a time. He saw the potential in me instead of the weakness.

He showed up to every volunteer meeting (sometimes he was the only one); he showed up at every outreach and every prayer meeting. He even had conversations with disgruntled people and told them not to give up on this young pastor, that God was doing something in him.

It's amazing how a person who just won't give up on you can define your future. Looking back at any success we've had, we often find that it was a teacher, a coach, a mentor, a parent, or someone who loved us beyond our ways that put just enough wind to our backs that we could carry on. The Dream Center exists because Gus, an eighty-year-old man, embraced an unqualified leader.

When you look at someone's accomplishments, there's always someone standing in the shadows who believed in that person's future. And we're called to be the kind of people that make dreams happen.

five

MISFITS AND ENCOURAGEMENT

We've talked a lot in this book about encouraging others, helping people, and serving even when you feel unprepared. As mentioned earlier, when we are living to make a difference in the world, we will often feel like misfits. The question people ask me the most is, "How do you stay encouraged to keep doing what you are doing?" How does someone stay motivated to help others who are in need?

One day I was reading the Word of God, and I came across a scripture that changed my life. It was 1 Samuel 30:6: "And David was greatly distressed; for the people spake of stoning him" (KJV).

Now, you know you've had a bad day when people are gathering a mob to try to kill you. I can see why David would be discouraged. We might think we have it bad, but it's not this bad.

The verse continues, "The soul of all the people was grieved, every man for his sons and for his daughters: but David encouraged himself in the LORD his God."

When I read that, it shot like a laser beam into my spirit. "David encouraged himself in the LORD." That is, as opposed to encouraging himself based on what the people thought of him. The quickest way to retirement is to live for man's appreciation. Do we love to feel appreciated? Sure. Do we love it when people honor what we do? Absolutely! Should it be a force in our choices and our lives moving forward? No.

Here's a great way to live life: Do everything unto the glory of God, and anything you get from man is a bonus. People can't always give you what you need. That's why serving for the honor and glory of God is the ultimate pursuit. Every time I've wanted to quit, it's because I didn't feel appreciated by man. The worst thing about pity parties is that we are usually the only ones who show up. David encouraged himself; he had a counseling session with himself to keep going.

Pressure can either cause us to break down, or it can cause us to find perspective. Look at the life of Nelson Mandela, who was exiled to Robben Island for his fight against apartheid. He was only allowed to meet with the outside world for thirty minutes a year. Prison allowed him to either get bitter or better. He came out better. He learned how to encourage himself in the prison, and it made him great. He even gave asylum to the people who put him in prison and led the world in the message of hope, love, and reconciliation.

The same thing happened in the life of King David. The prophet Samuel anointed him as a little shepherd boy, while taking care of sheep. Imagine you are just doing your job, and suddenly you're told out of the blue that you will be the king of Israel one day. Talk about an ordinary day turned great.

Then, all this was confirmed by signs and wonders. He took on the giant Goliath even though he was just a little ruddy shepherd boy. And he won! The nation was singing songs about this guy. But suddenly, his life changed courses. A jealous King Saul one day hurled a javelin at David while David was playing the harp to try to soothe the emotional distress of the unstable king. With that, David went from hero to fugitive. Running for his life, he ended up in a cave.

The Bible says,

> David departed from there and escaped to the cave of Adullam. And when his brothers and all his father's house heard it, they went down there to him. And everyone who was in distress, and everyone who was in debt, and everyone who was bitter in soul, gathered to him. (1 Sam. 22:1–2 ESV)

These were not the kind of people he was expecting to be surrounded by as the anointed king of Israel. How in the world had fortune turned this quickly? He thought he was heading for the throne, but he was hiding in a cave instead.

But David had to go through the cave to get to the palace. He learned three things in the cave: how to pray, how to praise, and how to persevere. In other words, he learned to encourage himself. On the surface, he had nothing to praise God about while hiding in the cave. So he looked on the inside and realized that if he really wanted, he could always find something to praise God for. He started to praise God not for what he could see but for who his God was.

> I will praise you, LORD, among the nations;
>   I will sing of you among the peoples.
> For great is your love, reaching to the heavens;
>   your faithfulness reaches to the skies. (Ps. 57:9–10)

> I cry to you, LORD;
>   I say, "You are my refuge,
>   my portion in the land of the living." (Ps. 142:5)

The same will work for us: deciding that we will allow God to be God is absolutely liberating. Don't praise Him for what you can see; praise Him that He's simply God, and that even in the cave He has a plan. As a matter of fact, the cave is often where He's preparing us to be stronger for the palace later.

■

The practical question still remains: How do you stay encouraged? When you feel like a misfit and you are taking on something that is far greater than your ability, how do you stay on the right track? I choose to rejoice in every small victory on the way to where I'm going. This ministry can be discouraging at times. We can pour our lives into people in our rehab program only to see them leave and go back out on drug binges. We can rescue trafficking victims only to see them go back to their pimps. It can make you go crazy, but only if you let it.

In twenty years of living a wild journey, I've learned that appreciating and celebrating little successes makes all the difference. I remember when we bought the massive hospital that would become the Dream Center. We had no money, but we decided we were going to renovate one room for a couple of guys in our rehab program to reside in. It wasn't a complete renovation of the hospital—we still had 397,000 square feet to occupy—but we raised money, prayed, and renovated our first 3,000 square feet.

When we were done, we had a party where we celebrated and acted like it was the greatest day of our lives. In that moment, we took the time to appreciate that little success, even though we had a lot more work to do to complete the vision. It took us eighteen more years to finish this hospital.

People look at the Dream Center today and say, "Wow! What an overnight success." Not even close. It's been inch-by-inch, room-by-room. Learning to celebrate small victories is the best way to stay encouraged in any walk of life. If we can't learn to enjoy the journey, we will never appreciate the arrival. Set some small goals on the way to the big ones. Enjoy every little victory along the way. In fact, make a big deal about small things and each little bit of ground gained on your journey. You can rejoice the rest of your life if you realize God is a God of the small victories as well as the big ones.

My father is a man who really knows how to appreciate the small things and get excited about them. Even though he's approaching eighty, every year he gets more animated about the life he lives. He continues to find meaning in everything, and that keeps him going.

One day a bunch of us guys were walking to see a friend of ours play golf on a PGA tour event here in Los Angeles at the famous Riviera Country Club. He's a pro golfer named Aaron Baddeley. We were all excited to be able to witness this important event. My father went with us, and we were cutting it close on time. We had to park in a nearby neighborhood, so it was a long walk from there to the golf course. Every step was getting faster and faster.

When we were almost there, we passed a house that had a beautiful flower garden. We rushed past it; we didn't have time to stop and smell the roses—we were going to watch our friend play some professional golf! Then, true to form, my father yelled, "Hey, guys! Did you see that flower garden?" I said, "Yes, Dad, it's beautiful." He called out again, "Did you really see it?" I shouted back, "Yes!" Then he ordered us back to the garden. "Come back here, boys."

We were clearly annoyed at his demand, but we walked back to the garden anyway. He said, "Stop! Look at how beautiful these flowers are." Then he unloaded on us. "You boys need to take more time to stare at how beautiful this is." And so we stood there staring at the garden for about ten minutes, until my father released us from garden jail.

We made it to the match, just a little late, but the powerful lesson we learned from my dad that day was more important. Don't just take time to smell the flowers, but to appreciate little things on the way to the big things. Little things keep you encouraged. Big events only come around infrequently, but little things can keep you encouraged all the time. Open your eyes to the little things, and you will maintain a life of consistent encouragement.

■

There's a young man in my church who is my go-to guy whenever I need encouragement. He's mentally handicapped, but I've never seen a young man praise God like he does. During worship he jumps up and down and cries at the same time. He's the only person I've ever met who has achieved total abandonment in worship.

Sometimes I'll be worrying about the order of service or if the music is just right or about some little technical glitch. When I start becoming an observer instead of a worshipper, I look back at my little buddy, jumping up and down praising with so much fervor, as if he's already in heaven. When I preach and make a good point, he will raise his Bible and stand up and affirm the preacher. "Amen, Pastor," he declares. He's locked into every moment with gratitude.

When I preach, my eyes always end up on that seat at the end of the aisle where my buddy cheers me on. When he prays, he wraps his arms around himself in such a beautiful way. I long to be as passionate as he is. He reminds me to get excited about the little things in life, whether in a crowd at church or alone on the road.

I spend the most time alone when I'm on the road raising money for the Dream Center through speaking tours. Every cent we raise on the road goes to support the Dream Center and the precious people there. So I travel a lot. I usually don't get back to the hotel until eleven o'clock at night. There's nobody in my room to say, "You did a good job." My buddy isn't there with an "Amen, Pastor" to cheer me on.

There are times, when you're all alone, that you just have to encourage yourself in the Lord. Remind yourself of God's faithfulness. As Lamentations says, "Because of the LORD's great love we are not consumed, for his compassions never fail. They are new every morning; great is your faithfulness" (3:22–23).

We get so preoccupied wanting God to do the next thing for us that we forget to thank Him for His past history of pulling us through. Looking back is a great way to be encouraged moving forward. A glimpse to the past can remind you of a God that was bigger than our past concerns and is bigger than what we are facing today. The quiet, reflective seasons of our lives really shape our destiny.

Most of life is slugging it out among the ordinary,

mundane days. Those days may seem like meaningless stops on the way to something better, but ordinary days are very powerful. They are a bridge that connects us to the future.

■

Sometimes encouragement comes by encouraging others. Over the years, I've learned to serve the hardest when I'm feeling the most selfish; that helps me press through to the other side. One Saturday I was trying frantically to find my sermon for the next day. I know, the thirteenth commandment of being a pastor is, "Thou shalt not wait until Saturday to finish your sermon." But I couldn't make it work.

I tried to find an old sermon and put on a new title to preach on Sunday. I looked through all the "greatest hits" sermons of my pastor friends, hoping to get inspiration from one of them. I picked up the Bible and started reading it, hoping to find a scripture to ignite the perfect inspiration. All that effort came to nothing—absolutely nothing. Saying I was frustrated is an understatement. I was lost. Lost in the mind-set of getting the next thing done. Just reacting rather than living.

In the midst of my panic, God began to speak into my spirit these words: "Forget about finding a sermon and go play kick ball with the kids out on Adopt-a-Block." Adopt-a-Block is a program where everyone in our church is encouraged to take one block of the city and serve the people who live there. We visit the people, ask them if they need anything, and just make ourselves available to serve. It's a lifetime commitment to that one area of the city.

We serve more than 150 blocks a week, and most of them we have been visiting for more than a decade. Some of our block leaders were talking about playing kick ball in a housing project right next to the central prison. Remembering how excited my Adopt-a-Block team was to love on the kids, I decided to forget about my sermon and go play kick ball.

I arrived at the housing project as a pastor without a sermon. I walked onto the ball field in the projects, sought out my Adopt-a-Block team, and screamed out, "I'm ready to play!" I could see the central prison looming over the field. One little boy told me his brother lived up there, chuckling as if it really wasn't a big deal. These kids were constantly faced with that harsh reality, but we had a chance to play in spite of it.

After the kick ball game was over, we ordered pizza for all the kids, and everyone had a great time. This day went from horrible, isolated panic to pure, serving bliss. Just hours before I'd been a paranoid pastor in his office worrying about what he'd look like if his message went flat the next day, but by some miracle I found myself sitting on a ball field eating pizza after a kick ball game with the beautiful children of East Los Angeles.

God needed me to get out of my selfishness before I could be encouraged to find the sermon He wanted me to preach. That wasn't going to happen if I kept stewing in my own juices, depending on myself to manufacture inspiration from my own power. In this case, my encouragement came from encouraging others. It's a cycle: the world needs you to be encouraged so you can breathe life back into it. Break away from anything that draws you back into the shell of self.

You will find life often requires a change of scenery. You can't be annoyed if you're not thinking about yourself. Next time you feel like you are swimming in the sea of discouragement, find a way to throw someone else a lifeline. Next time you feel entitled, frustrated, or at the limits of yourself, leap to your feet and do something to help others. It's the quickest way out of grief, pain, and the entitlement of selfishness. When feeling like a misfit, encourage yourself by finding a need and filling it, and finding a hurt and healing it.

six

MISFIT DREAMS

One of the greatest days of my life was the day I decided to die to my dream of being a success and become alive to the dream of being a blessing. There is no greater place to live than in the simplicity of that reality.

I used to be a pastor who would have ulcers if the crowd was down or if we had a month of low attendance. If people didn't show up, I would take it personally. One night on a prayer walk in Echo Park, God changed all that. God placed in my heart a simple thought: *You can't always control your position, but you can control your disposition. You can control your attitude. Love your city, love your community, and let Me build your church.* When you let go of a dream you thought you've always wanted and you give your efforts to God, you might feel out of control. *God, how can I live for something I can't control?* This scripture has become my life verse:

> *Trust in the LORD with all your heart,*
> *And lean not on your own understanding;*

In all your ways acknowledge Him,
And He shall direct your paths. (Prov. 3:5–6 NKJV)

Twelve words changed my life! "In all your ways acknowledge Him, and He shall direct your paths." I was standing on the wrong side of the dream. I was trying to direct my path, and God simply wanted me to acknowledge Him. I cut out twelve pieces of paper and put one word on each piece of paper. I taped a line down the middle of an empty room in my apartment and placed six words on one side, "In all your ways acknowledge Him," and on the other side of the line, "And He shall direct your paths." That room with those twelve words was a physical reminder of what side of the dream I was supposed to stand on.

God was the One to direct my path; I was simply to acknowledge Him. From then on, my life was never to be the same. My dreams took on a totally different form: my new pursuit was falling in love with Jesus, and using whatever He decided to give me to help others.

Once I had this change in perspective, God opened up doors. Our ministry started with one little donated apartment unit, and today we own a hospital with hundreds of rooms. The dream is so far from my initial playbook. In fact, I tell people the Dream Center is the world's greatest audible play. It doesn't fit into the portfolio and strategy I prepared before coming into this city. It keeps unfolding out of simple love, simple service, and openness.

People really become dangerous to the devil not when they see their dreams come into focus, but when they unlock dreams in their hearts they never knew they had—dreams that can only come about through serving. I am totally unqualified for every single assignment of my life, and that's what makes life exciting. You stop hoping for miracles and start depending on them.

■

One day a lady came to the Dream Center to get a tour of the facility. She and her husband lived in the Colorado area and were very successful in business. She had some free time and wanted to come over and see what we were up to.

We took her on a tour, and she met one of the girls who lived at our teen recovery home who gave a testimony of how her life was changed. This girl had been raised on the streets of Skid Row with her sister. The very thought of any child being raised on Skid Row is beyond comprehension.

The lady was moved. She had never in her life heard stories like this. Some of the kids live off the scraps of the streets— "Dumpster diving," they call it—while Mom and Dad are out day and night getting high. The kids are jammed up in a little hotel surrounded by drug deals and prostitution. After the lady heard the girls' testimonies, she headed back home, but the kids' stories never left her heart.

She called us a few days later. "I want to do something

special for all these girls for Christmas," she said. She asked us to book a restaurant for the girls to have a nice Christmas meal. I was about to reserve a spot at Denny's for the kids, but this generous woman would have none of that.

"Pastor," she said, "book a very nice, expensive place for these girls." She was almost mad at me for not thinking of booking the very best for these girls.

We found a place in Hollywood connected to a fancy hotel that fit the bill. We drove our old Dream Center bus down the highway with forty teenagers who lived at the center, and met our beaming sponsor at the door. The girls walked into the restaurant with a look of total amazement on their faces. They were not taken aback by the moment—they were taken over. One girl started to cry. Another was trying to figure out what a menu was; she never had been to a restaurant in her entire life.

The forty girls enjoyed that feast like children at Willy Wonka's chocolate factory. I thanked our gracious host for flying all the way from Colorado for this, and to my surprise she had another gift. Certainly, this pricey lunch was enough? No.

The lady handed a bag to each of the girls and told them to open the bags. The cute little gift bags were torn apart, revealing five hundred dollars to go shopping. Five hundred dollars for each girl! This day wasn't over. It was heating up.

The gift took their breath away. "This is the first time I've ever seen a hundred dollar bill legally," said one girl. Another went to the corner and cried.

Now it was time to go shopping. Off I went to the mall

with forty teenage girls for seven hours. I'd rather spend seven years in the tribulation than seven hours with a teenage girl at the mall. But this time was special.

One girl went to Forever 21 and bought as many things as she could buy under five dollars. She wanted to make sure that if this was her only chance to shop, she was going to load up. Another girl wouldn't buy anything because she wanted to spend the money on her father who was in prison. Finally, I convinced her to enjoy the shopping spree.

Shopping with these girls was something I'll never forget. They would buy something at a store and then just cry. They couldn't believe something so beautiful was happening to them.

When the shopping spree was over, we went back to the Dream Center. The girls tried on their clothes, modeled them, and did a little fashion show in the living room. You could tell they didn't know much about fashion. Who cares! It was their day, their money, their experience.

Then we sat around talking, and one of the girls asked me a question. "Pastor," she asked, "what is your dream?" The question took me by surprise, and to be honest I answered it incorrectly. I gave them the typical corporate answer—numbers and square footage we wanted to remodel at the center. It wasn't my real dream; it was just a typical rehearsed answer to sound like I knew what I was doing. She seemed disappointed my dream was so well rehearsed and, frankly, shallow.

I drove home that night weeping with joy. I got to go shopping with forty girls (many of whom were practically orphans) and see twenty thousand dollars spent on kids who would otherwise never get that chance. It was one of the best days of my ministry.

A few days later I saw the young lady who asked me about my dream. "Can I have a second chance at that answer?" I asked. She said yes. "All right, then here's my dream," I started. "My dream is to make sure your dream comes true."

She smiled. "Pastor, that's the best answer ever."

■

Misfit dreamers want to see other people's dreams come true. They go to work for a purpose; they generate money for a purpose. They use their influence to dream for people who have lost their dreams.

There are many conferences in the business world and church world that try to teach us how to gain influence. Everyone wants influence. Why? So we can have power to move more pawns around in our quest for power? Servant-hearted dreamers fall in love with giving their lives away. Life is simple: make life better for others with whatever you have in hand.

I'm typing this book on the eighth floor of the Dream Center hospital. I can hear the sound of the 101 Hollywood Freeway below me humming along. Moving my chair to the right, I can see from my window the lights of downtown Hollywood. It's an intriguing setting to write a book about dreams, with such a contrasting view in my sight.

Most people come to this city to become something big. Most do not find what they are looking for. The Hollywood dream becomes a nightmare. Some do find what they are looking for, but then discover after the endless accumulation that their dream is empty and provides no outlet by which to express real joy. Celebrities who have attended our charity events say things like, "This was the best experience of my life." Or, "I've lived in Los Angeles for years and never seen this side of the city."

Influence only feels complete when there's an object of real value attached to it. Influence is pointless if it's not lifting people up along the journey. More people fail because they don't know how to handle success than those who fail from failure.

Every person needs a mission—something to live for. We can achieve all our goals and still miss the mark. We can help our kids succeed in school and watch them flounder trying to make it. Here's the truth: we were born to serve, born to make a difference, born to use our influence for good.

■

Let me tell you about a person who understood influence.

Josh Lindblom is a major-league baseball player with the Los Angeles Dodgers. During home games, he would stop by the Dream Center and do street outreaches several times a week before going to the stadium. Folks, this wasn't a cameo appearance; it was a way of life. Josh would go to Skid Row, serve food, even get yelled at sometimes, then head to Dodger Stadium to pitch an incredible season. It was a season to remember.

Major League baseball season is 162 games a year. Even making it out to help us one day a year would be a kind gesture. Not Josh. He was addicted—addicted to serving! He made such an impact on the Dream Center that one night he arranged for all our men and women at the Dream Center to go to the Dodgers game. And I mean *all*. Josh made it possible for hundreds of Dream Center people to fill the stands that night.

The Dodgers were up by one run in the eighth inning, which meant it was time for Josh to come in. When Josh ran to the mound, the cameras focused on the section of people he had supplied with tickets. It was such a moving sight. Guys and girls in our rehab program, screaming homeless families. Everyone, many of whom Josh had directly helped, was jumping up and down. I cheered so loud I had a headache.

Why were we cheering? Were we cheering because we are Dodger fans? Okay, maybe just a little. But the real reason we were cheering is because Josh was the people's champion, the advocate of the underdog, the man who loved the city of Los Angeles, the man who showed us that success was not given to us to rule—it was given to us to serve. He reminded us that the greater the influence you have, the greater the calling to lift up others.

The Dream Center people were not cheering for Josh as an athlete; they were cheering for Josh the servant. What happened when he got into the game? Josh retired every batter in order—one, two, three—in a dominating performance. There's no other way it could have gone. Once again, Josh was making everyone else's day brighter. Josh has moved on to another team, but his example of using influence for the least of these will never die.

■

Misfit dreamers make time in their schedules to make a difference. We all have jobs, occupations, to earn money. It's a part of life we can never discount. It's just that some people find a way, or make a way, to include making a difference as a core value in all they do. They live by the strategy of hope.

Live in the awareness that simple things make a big difference. Have you ever done something for someone that seemed small to you, but to them it was a big deal? You have shocked them with kindness.

We live in a world that says, "Get what you want at any cost even if you have to step on some people to get there." Instead ask, "Who can I bring along with me as I succeed in this life?" It doesn't make sense to the common man, but misfit dreamers are not common. They are selfless, and they realize life is only truly lived when we carry others toward their dreams.

Tucked away in the housing projects of Los Angeles is a lady named Graciela. Graciela has been living in the projects since the 1980s. Graciela is in her eighties. One day in her sixties, Graciela woke up blind. She'd lost her sight.

Around her everywhere are gangs, drug dealers, and robbers. Being alone in the projects and hearing the sounds of robberies, gang violence, and chaos is a brutal way for a blind senior citizen to live. She has some family who check on her now and then, but a majority of her day she spends alone trying to navigate the large stairway that leads to her small apartment upstairs.

My wife, Caroline, visits her once a week. She told me about this remarkable woman, so one day I decided to join my wife in a visit to her house. The run-down apartment was immaculately clean. Everything was in place. Graciela can't see, but she certainly can feel. She knows exactly where everything needs to be.

My wife brings her papaya and other groceries every Saturday. Graciela returns the favor and makes us spicy black beans from a recipe straight out of her Guatemalan homeland. They are so good and my wife now has her famous recipe.

On this particular occasion, when we visited Graciela, she spoke of God's presence being so near. Graciela ran from one story to the next because she didn't want the visit to end. Interested in how she filled her time, I asked what she did all week.

"I can't always tell time, so basically I sit here in this chair all week waiting for the door to ring," she said. "Caroline, the only reason I stay alive is because I wait for your visit."

Talk about heartbreaking. I think in all the years I've been in ministry, this is the saddest statement I've ever heard. Here's a blind lady who basically sits on a chair all week long just to wait for my wife to come to her house to talk to her. It's the only thing left she has to live for. My wife is extremely busy and can speak almost anywhere she wants in the country, but she always takes time to visit Graciela.

When my wife and I talk about ministry, we always say that if the church ever got tired of us being their pastors we would just sign up and volunteer at the Dream Center. Life is never too fast paced to love people one-on-one. It's imperative we make a way to fit serving into the pace of our lives. We make time for the things we value.

As we grow older, we are taught to hold on to things. Hold on to power, control, protect what is ours. To live life that way is just out of the bounds of reality and responsibility. If we do that, we change into someone who simply tries to protect what they have instead of giving it away. We learn how to protect our own dreams; we read books on how to stay ahead of everyone else. The entire goal is to spend life trying to rise above the pack.

That's not the purpose of our lives. The purpose of life is not to be a dream holder but to be a dream maker. I have learned that no one has ever made their own dreams come true by trying to hold on to them, but by making the dreams of others come true.

A dream holder will defend his turf, defend what he wants, be happy as long as everyone fits into his world. A dream maker will only be happy when she defends the cause of what others want. A dream holder is like King Saul, the enemy of David, who says, "How can I hold back others who are challenging me from behind?" A dream maker says, "How can I make the people around me better?" A dream holder says, "You will conform to me." A dream maker says, "I will conform to you."

■

Growing up as a pastor's son, I went through a season of my life where I was disillusioned with the ministry. I had seen so much hypocrisy that I was starting to get judgmental. My grandmother was a great counselor before she passed away. She was the kind of lady who held your hand in such a loving way you could tell her anything.

"Grandma," I said one day, "I'm so fed up with hypocritical Christians." My grandmother, in the sweetest and yet firmest voice I've ever heard, told me, "The problem with you is that you are looking for an example. Stop looking for an example— and be an example."

Her comments came down like thunder and lightning. Then she added one more bolt. "Be what you want the world to be," she said. If you want the world to be optimistic, you become optimistic. What do you do when your dream seems so far away? Make someone else's dream come true. Serve their dream while you are on the way toward yours.

Whatever we make happen for others seems to always come back to us. While pursuing God's plan for your life, help someone else who is closer than you are. Or, if you've already advanced far in your calling, bring someone else along. Live to be a blessing. Always be pushing someone or pulling someone to go higher, like the runners I saw at a Special Olympics track meet.

The gun went off and the runners were sprinting to the finish line. One of the runners fell to the ground. Suddenly all the other runners stopped, ran back to the fallen runner, and picked him up. Something was so beautiful about that scene. There was no trophy worth more than going back and helping a fallen brother. While pursuing your calling, don't forget to pick up people who have fallen along the way.

seven

MISFITS HELPING MISFITS

I t was a sight we will never forget.

In our recovery home we have people from every walk of life—people of different races, people from gangs, and folks from every type of background. One of our guys walked into one of the rooms where the men live and saw a former skinhead, a former Crip from South Central, and a young man involved with Latino gangs from East LA, all praying together in the same room. They had their arms around each other, praying.

It was truly a remarkable sight. This is something you would never expect to see. However, Jesus breaks down walls. The men were not just tolerating one another, they were brothers. The world would view each of these men as criminals and permanently labeled because of their backgrounds. But now we've come to realize that when you believe in misfits and dream for misfits, they start helping other misfits. The entire New Testament story line is outcasts helping one another. Good news travels fast!

I love it when people take chances on underdogs. I love it when I see a business give a job to someone who would be overlooked by others, when a college gives a former criminal a second chance and a shot at education.

It's undeniable that Jesus was not afraid to believe in misfits, and it's inspiring to see how they were a part of His plan of transformation. The Bible Hall of Fame makes some people scratch their heads. True, the list includes prostitutes, murderers, and fornicators. But look at what many of these people did after getting their second chances.

Samson tore down pillars in the temple after losing his hair, having his eyes gouged out, and being labeled "washed up." His greatest victory came at the moment he was labeled finished. Peter denied Jesus, but forty days later he was preaching on the day of Pentecost.

■

One day, on our Adopt-a-Block weekly visitation, I knocked on a door during the regular rounds of service. An elderly Filipino gentleman greeted me kindly and told me to come in. You could tell this man didn't have a lot of people coming over to see him. I told him we were just coming by to check on him to make sure he was fine. If he needed anything, he could just track us down and we were ready to serve him.

He said, "I know a way you can help me." I thought for sure he was going to want us to paint his apartment or help him move furniture. But he said, "Would you mind doing a Bible study with me on the love of God?" I almost laughed at the request because I didn't expect it.

For ten weeks I read this old Filipino war veteran the Bible and talked to him about the love of God. Then, on the last week, I told him, "Your homework is to go out and help someone else." The next week I knocked on the door and he answered, putting his finger over his mouth signaling me to be quiet. I asked what was wrong.

He said, "I saw this family that was homeless walking down the street." He whispered even quieter, "I remember you talking about the love of God and about how I need to help someone else." I looked at the family he took into his apartment, and it was tragic. They had no shoes, were rail thin, and had been traveling for days to get to this country.

The man told me, "Pastor, please be quiet, because they are staying with me and I don't think they're legal citizens." I felt like saying, "Don't worry—this is Los Angeles. You are probably going to be okay." The elderly gentleman acted on my Bible study. He actually took in this family that just came across the border and gave them a place to stay. The man shocked me by responding so drastically to my challenge of helping someone else. I'm used to church where sometimes the things I say can go in one ear and out the other. This man was doing something about what he learned.

My Bible study friend said, "Do we have any clothes for this family?" Talk about a God who orchestrates events. We had just got in a shipment of brand-new clothes from Guess jeans. The clothes we were giving away still had the price tags on them. We called the Dream Center campus and asked them to run supplies over to this apartment. The family was lavished with love and an incredible wardrobe of coats and jeans valued at hundreds of dollars.

The man who had just come to America was so moved by this experience that he went over to the corner of the room, put his hands on his face, and in Spanish said, "I've only been in America for a few hours and a man gave me a place to stay, and the church has brought me clothes." He continued, "Wow! What a country! Is everyone like this over here?" I didn't want to burst his bubble. "Oh yeah," I said, while thinking, *Let's let reality hit him later.*

The point of this story is that this unlikely older gentleman helped a weary traveling family who were clearly misfits in a new country. People helping people creates a ripple effect. The multiplication in helping someone could cause a chain reaction of miracles. Misfits turned on to God become an inspiration.

■

Let me tell you about a man who is one of the greatest miracles I've ever encountered. His name is Barry, and he was born in Michigan in 1951. From the earliest time he can remember until he was seven years old, he was locked in the upper attic of his home. He never really saw his parents, who, he would later find out, were actually his grandparents. He was told he had nine brothers and sisters but only saw one of them during those first years. His sister would bring him food in the attic and help him out if he needed anything. Despite this, she abused him all seven years, verbally and physically.

Barry thought this was how every child was raised. He had no friends and was never allowed to come out of the attic. At age seven, his grandparents (whom at the time he still thought were his parents) enrolled him in a Catholic school. They moved him from the attic to the hallway. They had no room for him, so he lived in the open passageway. His sister had moved out of the house, but he met his other brothers and sisters who lived together in other rooms. Barry was very smart and was always top of his class despite all the abuse he had suffered. He started taking drugs, however, at age eleven to cope with the pain of his childhood.

In tenth grade Barry left school to join the navy. By this time he was addicted to several drugs. When he went to the navy, he was introduced to heroin. He was in the navy for one year and then received an honorable discharge. He came back to Michigan, addicted to drugs, but wanted to finish high school. At age twenty he went back to his high school, attended classes, and graduated at age twenty-one. While he was in high school, he worked part-time for his brother at a supply shop. He stole from his brother for drugs.

Barry applied to Michigan State University and received a

full academic scholarship to study civil engineering. He stayed for a semester and transferred to Cass Tech and went there three years before getting a job as a general foreman at a steel mill. He worked there for five years, still strung out on drugs. He met a woman and married her. They had two children, but when he realized his drug abuse was affecting them, he ran.

Barry came out to California and got a job working for the Farr Company, which makes air-filtration products. It was at that point he received a revelation that changed his life. At forty years old, Barry finally discovered the reason he was locked in the attic until he was seven.

One of his brothers, who was dying of cancer, flew out to see him. He said he needed to tell Barry something before he died. He said the girl Barry thought was his sister, the abusive one who visited him in the attic, was really his mom. One of the brothers in the house had raped his sister, and Barry was conceived. Barry's grandparents were so ashamed that they hid him in the attic until his mother moved out of the house.

There was no way Barry could talk to his real mom or dad, because they were already deceased. His biological mom had died when he was twenty-four, and his father had committed suicide.

Barry was devastated over this family secret. But things started to make sense; he now knew why he was locked in the attic. Because of the pain and hurt, Barry started using meth and lost his job and house. He ended up homeless in Harbor City, California, living under a bridge.

Barry lived homeless under a bridge for seventeen years. He went from Dumpster to Dumpster to survive. In 2005 a woman met Barry and took him some food. She invited him to her church to get help, and after a couple of weeks thinking about it, he decided to visit. The kids in the church called him the Bridge Troll because of his hair (which was down to his waist), his dirty clothes, and beard.

The pastor of the church told Barry about the Dream Center. He told him there was a program here that could help straighten out his life. Barry had been addicted to meth for all these years but was ready to change. Three days before Barry was to come to the Dream Center and enter the men's discipleship program, he was arrested for living under the bridge. Barry went to jail but got out on bond. He entered the men's home three days later and never thought again about the court date for his hearing (more on that later).

Barry lived for two years in the men's home and has been completely clean from drugs for six years. He wanted to go to Bible school, so we at the Dream Center funded his way. Barry has been working at the Dream Center for six years. He recently completed his pastoral license and is a supervisor for the food outreach at the Dream Center.

Barry helps feed two thousand hot meals a day to the homeless men and women in recovery at the Dream Center, to homeless families, to girls being rescued from human trafficking, and to many more. In the mornings and evenings, Barry also holds chapel services for the homeless. He shares his story of transformation and encourages all the homeless that they, too, can overcome their situations and live for something greater.

A couple of days ago, Barry had to go to court over the ticket he received for living under the bridge. He had forgotten all about the ticket, and they had a warrant out for his arrest. When he met with the judge, she looked through everything Barry has accomplished in the last six years and how he is living each day devoted to his new cause of bringing the homeless off the street. She stood in the courtroom and started clapping. Everyone in the courtroom gave him a standing ovation, and she said all charges were dropped because she had never heard a more amazing story of change.

The incredible thing is that now Barry is plucking people one by one from under the bridges of Los Angeles and bringing them toward a better life. Barry was the kind of man whom many of us drive by and say, "That person is too far gone to change." Honestly, I've said that in the past. But when God gets ahold of someone's life, anything is possible.

■

One of the things we teach people at the Dream Center is to never waste their pain. There is value in your struggle, just as there was a miraculous value in Barry's struggle. Maybe you are thinking about all the pain in your life, in your past, and wondering how God can possibly redeem it.

My advice is to use your pain for something great. Let your struggle be somebody else's freedom. There is redemption behind pain. The fact you are even striving to overcome is a blessing to someone who may be considering even the possibility of trying.

This big old hospital has been built as a beacon of hope by a bunch of people who presented their pain to God. We've seen God turn it into something glorious. God can use our pain, because in our pain we learn how to rely on the "power of His might" (Eph. 6:10 NKJV). There are people, rich and poor, in every city who feel disqualified because of their mistakes. It's our job as redeemed misfits to encourage current misfits to get back up again and start to make a difference.

■

The day before I had to turn in the manuscript for this book, I prayed, "God, if there's any last-minute thing you want to add to this book, let it be done." A few hours before the deadline, a man we'll call Alex gave a testimony at church. He was facing a fifteen-year prison sentence for attempted murder. He had tried to kill a man in a gang fight and the man was paralyzed. The man he shot would be in a wheelchair for the rest of his life.

Alex had been in our recovery program for a few months waiting for his court date, waiting to be locked away. Some of his family had told him to flee the country. Shockingly, Alex didn't take the offer of the plane ticket to Mexico. He decided to stay in the country, in our program, and as he said, "Man up to the consequences." He arrived in the courtroom thinking it was the end of the road for him. *Fifteen-to-life in prison, here we come.*

The prosecution entered the courtroom, and the man in the wheelchair asked to say something. He told Alex that he was dropping all the charges against him. He told him, "At first I was mad at you for shooting me and paralyzing me." Then he said, "When you shot me, it took my legs away. It was also the day I decided to leave the gangs. I never would have left the gangs if you wouldn't have shot me." He forgave Alex and set him free. Alex was astonished by the lavish grace of this man.

After Alex finished speaking, I stood up on stage and told him that he had received a second chance and now it was time to extend that grace to every single person he met for the rest of his life—the same grace the man who dropped all the charges gave him.

This miraculous story is much like the apostle Paul's story, when you think of it. Paul, or Saul, as he was called in his younger years, was a misfit. In fact, he was a man who persecuted the church, hated the church, and even saw people executed who stood boldly for the church. Let's take a look at the transformation of this man from Saul to Paul.

Meanwhile, Saul was still breathing out murderous threats against the Lord's disciples. He went to the high priest and asked him for letters to the synagogues in Damascus, so that if he found any there who belonged to the Way, whether men or women, he might take them as prisoners to Jerusalem. As he neared Damascus on his journey, suddenly a light from heaven flashed around him. He fell to the ground and heard a voice say to him, "Saul, Saul, why do you persecute me?"

"Who are you, Lord?" Saul asked.

"I am Jesus, whom you are persecuting," he replied. "Now get up and go into the city, and you will be told what you must do." (Acts 9:1–6)

Saul, or Paul, was changed from a persecutor to a follower of Christ. How would this journey play out? How would he evolve from murderer to missionary? It would happen because of one man named Barnabas. Barnabas took Saul under his wing and believed Saul still had a future. He embraced him. The other disciples didn't want to be near him, they didn't trust him, but Barnabas saw the hidden man of the misfit's heart (Acts 9:26–27). This is what discipleship is all about. It's not about seeing how far people have to go; it's about walking by someone one step at a time.

■

My entire ministry team is a collection of castoffs. Maybe they're someone from a church that's failed. Maybe they're someone whose own family didn't want them, or who suffered public rejection. We always receive calls asking, "Can you take this wounded person?" One man said to me, "How does it feel to get all the discarded people?" My answer? "Wonderful." I am grateful that churches and families would give them to us.

Give me the castoffs. Give me the people who are in dire need of regenerative grace. Give me the people who haven't kept the religious handbook. Give me the ones who have been exiled to the ash heap of broken parts. I've grown to love castoffs because they have shown me an entirely new way to see life. I have been changed by these broken people.

The closer I get to helping others in their brokenness, the more broken I realize I am. I'm not better than the broken parts I try to put back together. I often feel equally battered. The reality is that we all pick each other up along the way.

The only people who came to church when I started were the people nobody wanted. Addicts, the marginalized, and even leaders who fell and were rejected by their own churches. My greatest honor is to be known as the pastor of these people. I'm thankful for them. I thought I would come to Los Angeles and save a bunch of people. The truth is, the castoffs saved me, restored me, and poured new life into my soul.

Misfits helping misfits works perfectly in God's plan. Barnabas took a risk in helping Paul, but the benefits were beyond incredible. The entire world was changed because of Paul's ministry. Yes, you might believe in someone and they might fail—or you could believe in someone and they could change the world like Paul. Fear of failure hinders us from finding that out. But when we invest full belief in misfits, it gives them confidence they can make it.

eight

MISFITS REDEEMED

I love this poem written about risk.

> *There once was a very cautious man,*
> *who never laughed or cried.*
> *He never cared, he never dared.*
> *He never dreamed or tried.*
> *And when one day he passed away,*
> *his insurance was denied.*
> *For since he never really lived,*
> *they claimed he never died.*

> —AUTHOR UNKNOWN

The beauty in believing in others is the possibility of the multiplication factor. When Jesus believed in people, restored them, forgave them, they immediately went and told everyone they knew what Jesus had done for them (Mark 7:36–8:1). How can you blame them? There's something so beautiful about giving a second chance at life to someone who thinks they've been cut off from ever truly living again.

I'll never forget the story of one of our staff who was going out to the streets of Skid Row to do outreach. He walked by a man sitting up against the wall and said, "Sir, we have free food down the street."

The man just stared at our volunteer with a glazed look in his eyes. Our volunteer once again repeated himself, "Sir, we have free food down the street."

The man shook off the cobwebs of indifference, stared at our worker, and said, "Are you talking to me? Oh, I thought I was invisible."

The man actually thought he was invisible. Every day, I wonder how many people feel invisible. In the office, in our schools, even in our marriages, sadly, many people feel invisible. They need a misfit to come along and help direct them to the life within them that they might see.

■

One of the most incredible servants I've ever met is a man by the name of Israel Martinez. One by one, I've seen layers of pain in his life be removed. Israel has gone from impossible odds to a glorious comeback. It all started with a six-hour walk out of desperation. Here's Israel's story, as he tells it.

Before coming to the Dream Center and surrendering my life over to Jesus Christ, I lived a life of confusion. I grew up in a Catholic family of five. Growing up, my father never enforced church attendance in the family, so you can say I never knew who God was, nor was I even interested in knowing Him at the time. The only thing I knew was that someone told me there was a God, but I was not saved. Neither did I have any knowledge about Him. As the years went on I began to grow curious about who God was. I began to seek for His truth through many different avenues. I didn't find the answer I was looking for.

I spent most of my youth running with a gang in the streets of South Central Los Angeles. At the age of fifteen, I met a young girl at a party, and we ended up dating. Within six months she became pregnant. This situation was too much pressure for me to handle at such a young age, so I ran from my responsibility as a father. In 1997, I was introduced to crystal methamphetamines, and this turned out to be the beginning of a twelve-year drug addiction. I ended up losing the little that I had at the time, and I quickly spiraled downhill. For a few years I sought professional help in secular recovery programs with no success.

In 2004, my cousin gave me a tour of the Dream Center. He offered for me to stay, but I refused because I didn't feel I was ready. In those days I was really struggling with my addiction, so I began to cry out to God in distress, sorrow, and pain. I would say things to Him like: "If You really exist, then take away my pain." At one point I even desired death.

One morning I was getting ready for work, and I had been up for two days without any sleep, food, or water. My friends stopped by and picked me up at home, and we drove off. On our way to work, we hit a traffic jam, and we were there for about forty-five minutes. I began to feel dizzy and weak, as if I was going to pass out, but then I remember a great fear coming upon me, as if I were going to die. At this time my friends began to get scared, and we exited the freeway immediately. They took me to a gas station and bought me some over-the-counter medication, but when I took it I got even worse. As I worsened I felt more fear, then I blanked out and the paramedics had to come pick me up.

After waking up in the hospital bed, I knew exactly where I needed to go. I never felt so eager to come to the Lord as I did on that day. After I left the hospital I ended up walking all the way from Westwood hospital to the Dream Center. It took me six hours on foot to get there. When I got to the Dream Center, I was dehydrated, my legs were hurting, my feet were blistered, and I was in weak physical shape, weighing only about 120 pounds.

I was spotted by a leader from the men's discipleship home. He asked if I needed help, and I told him yes. He then took me to the Dream Center discipleship chapel, and I will never forget the feeling that came over me that night. It is hard to explain, but let's just say I felt welcomed, accepted, and loved. I dropped to my knees and began to weep like never before. Then I was prayed for and taken into the discipleship program.

The next morning when I woke up I saw a Bible by my bed and began reading it. Two days later, on September 13, 2004, I surrendered and gave my life to the Lord. I can't remember a time in my life when I cried so much out of pure joy.

After having given my life to the Lord, I came to understand that God allowed me to wander in this direction so I could hit rock bottom, and turn to Him for help. I realized God had a calling for my life. Now that I have been saved, I feel like a new person. Before coming to the Lord, I thought I would never change who I used to be. As a matter of fact, I didn't think God Himself could ever set me free. For as long as I had been in my addiction, I thought I was going to die like that. I now look at Christianity like an awesome lifestyle, and I enjoy living for God.

Since I've given my life to the Lord and started serving at the Dream Center, God has done miracles in my life. I have cut off old friends who, at one point in my life, were influencing me to do the wrong things, and I have surrounded myself with people who influence me to succeed in life. In 1996, I had abandoned my son and his mom. I spent many years saddened by what I had done, then one day during a Sunday morning service, I felt God speak to me through a sermon by pastor Matthew Barnett titled "Facing Your Biggest Fears."

I was inspired by this message so much that I felt God press it upon my heart to go look for my son. I took action in 2008, and went before the judge in 2009 to formally seek the right to be part of my son's life. I was excited to hear the judge say, "Israel, we are granting you visitation rights." What had seemed impossible to me was not impossible to God. This was His way of showing me His goodness and greatness. God has united me with my son and is now restoring my relationship with him.

I graduated the first year of the discipleship program in 2007 and the second-year connections program in 2008, and was also fortunate to receive my GED at the Dream Center, as well as get my driver's license. I am currently on staff at the Dream Center working in the food ministry department as an assistant manager and serving as an usher at church. At the same time, I am currently attending Bible College at Angelus Bible Institute, and I will be graduating in June of 2014.

Now, after all these years, I feel God is preparing me to go out into the field and minister to people who have struggles and setbacks in life. God keeps presenting opportunities to me. Recently I have had the privilege of teaching the Word of God in different churches, and even leading Bible studies. It has been a blessing to serve here at the Dream Center and serve with great people and leaders. I am grateful to be a part of a church that helps people dream again.

The church can oftentimes be a place where we try to protect the culture we've created, even hide from the hurting, and act like they don't even exist. It's a huge risk to bring the most hurting into the church on Sunday because they might mess up our safe, respectable environment. Playing it safe is no way to win in the kingdom of God. Living on the edge has always been the call of the New Testament church.

Many people settle for playing it safe because they are so afraid of failing. Take a chance on risky people, and you could discover there's someone like an apostle Paul behind the flaws and the failure. The chain begins with one link. The belief you have in one person making it could possibly start a generation of misfits helping misfits. After Barnabas believed in Paul, Paul brought the gospel to new territories and people who were regarded as misfits—the Gentiles (Gal. 1:15–16). The revival spread, and our lives will never be the same again.

■

I want to introduce you to our children's pastor. My children don't know his testimony, or his backstory, but they love him.

One night before going to bed, I asked my seven-year-old son Caden what he wanted to be when he grew up. His answer? "I want to be Pastor Kenny." Here is Pastor Kenny's story.

To this day I'm still in awe of what God has done in and through my life, and how He has chosen to use me to help so many. I am living the scripture that those who are forgiven much love much (Luke 7:47).

I remember the day I decided that instead of going to school I was going to skip school and hang out with my friends and we went drinking. That was the beginning of a terrible spiral that led me so far down, it is only by the grace and mercy of Jesus that I am where I am today and in my right mind.

My life was such a mess that I was either going to die of a drug overdose or spend the rest of my life in prison. I became so addicted to drugs and alcohol that I did not care about anything or anyone and I lost everything, including my family and so many friends. One night I will never ever forget is the night I lost my friends Joyce and Jeff and their baby.

Joyce called me crying, saying I needed to come and pick her and the baby up because Jeff was so high he was going crazy. When I arrived I was too late. I walked into one of the most gruesome sights I have ever witnessed. Jeff had taken a gun and taken all their lives. I watched as the paramedics took them all out of the house. One of those paramedics was my own brother, who looked at me with disgust. He could not believe I dared to be there.

Even after that, my life did not change. It just got worse. I did not care about anyone or anything, including myself, and all I wanted was to die. I had been arrested so many times the courts labeled me hopeless and crazy. To this day my criminal record lists me as a 5150, a code used to refer to people who can be detained involuntarily when their obvious mental disturbance could be considered a threat to themselves or others.

My life was a mess, but I had a praying mom and sister. One day my brother-in-law came to visit me in jail and asked me if I wanted to make a change. He told me about a residential one-year recovery program for adults called Teen Challenge, and he told me Jesus loved me and wanted to forgive me. I was unsure about Jesus but I wanted to get better.

Once I got out of jail I went straight into Teen Challenge. There I met Jesus and graduated from their discipleship program and then their Bible institute in 1994. While in Bible school I became a children's pastor. I took an old ice cream truck and converted it into a mobile kids' church that pulls into the community. The side folds out and we have church services from the truck. We called it "sidewalk Sunday school."

After living such a crazy life, it was not an easy

process for me to think God could ever really use my life, even though I was serving in ministry. I felt He loved me but could not understand why He was choosing to use me. I felt underqualified, like I was never going to be good enough because of all I had done and all that had been spoken over my life.

It was hard for me to talk to people because I was scared that my words made no sense at all—a throwback to my previous unstable state. All I wanted to do was quit some days. Some days, the guilt and shame were so overwhelming that I felt I would never amount to anything!

Then one day I felt God speak to me through His Word, out of 1 Corinthians 1:27: "But God chose the foolish things of the world to shame the wise; God chose the weak things of the world to shame the strong." I realized God uses everyone, including me. I started to see that as I gave my life away, I felt healing and freedom come into my own life.

I was imperfect, but God chooses to use imperfect people to change the world. I didn't need to be qualified to help someone. I started to experience God's unconditional love and forgiveness and healing, which helped me move from the past to the present, where I walk in God's confidence.

Here I am twenty years later, and there is one thing I'm sure of: God uses ordinary people to do extraordinary things.

Today Pastor Kenny is bringing hope to the world. He has chosen to serve out of his pain and make a difference, showing us all that misfits helping misfits is the way God starts revolutionary change. The funny thing is that my kids don't even know Pastor Kenny's past. They think he's been a Christian all his life.

Have you heard the phrase, "I don't know you anymore"? This is what I see every day. People who have endured such pain and heartache washing all that pain away by serving someone else. When we throw ourselves into someone else's world, our world of misery gets smaller and smaller as we make someone else's world bigger and better.

I truly believe we can serve our way into freedom. There's never a good time to serve or a time we are more worthy to serve. We serve now, wherever we are, and in the process discover true freedom.

nine

MISFIT LOVE

Sometimes when you demonstrate love to someone you don't know, other people's reactions can be skeptical—even suspicious.

For instance, on airplanes, when we arrive at our destination and the signal goes off letting us know we have arrived, I like to get up immediately and start getting people's bags down for them. Something so simple as getting a bag usually draws suspicious looks and questions. "Why are you doing this?" or "What is your agenda?" It's a shame. We have become numb to the idea that anyone would want to do good for no reason.

But should we let that stop us? The other day I was at a mall standing in line at a Chick-fil-A to get those amazing chicken nuggets. A lady in front of me was one dollar short. She was trying to cut a deal by subtracting nuggets from her order. I told the lady I would buy her combo. She looked at me and said, "No one has ever done anything like that for me before." I replied, "They should, because you are a wonderful lady."

She shook her head and started to cry. It's amazing how little it takes to affect someone's life. People who show love don't fit in to the world's skeptical thinking. A person who operates in love doesn't think, *Maybe I'll offend them if I buy them food.* They just feel, respond, and love. Their love doesn't fit the mold. It's not typical, it's not everyday life, and it's what makes love so wonderful. It doesn't make sense, but it doesn't have to.

It's one thing to think of creative ideas. It's another thing to let love inspire your ideas. It's amazing how loving someone can cause us to look within ourselves and find skills to make someone's life better. Love opens the door to creative thinking. A lady at our church wanted to do a major outreach for the children of our neighborhood, but she had one problem: she didn't have much money. She did, however, have an idea. She decided to take cardboard boxes, shape them, and turn them into little designer cars big enough for a kid to sit in.

Imagine cardboard being shaped into a box, and then the box shaped into a Ferrari, truck, or Corvette, and then painted to complete the transformation. There you go! Cardboard has turned into "carsboard" (that's what we call it). She made rows and rows of these cars, and we started a drive-in movie theater right on the parking lot of the Dream Center. Little kids were watching a drive-in movie in their custom-made cardboard cars. The kids had popcorn and soda in their vehicles, and felt like hotshots for the day. All from cardboard and an idea.

Love generates crazy ideas that may seem simple but are

actually profound. Love causes us to think of some pretty crazy spontaneous plans too. You can plan ways to make a difference or just look at what you possess in your soul and use it as a gift.

■

If you don't believe that love inspires extreme creativity, just look at the dating process. When a man is in love, he will find a way to woo his woman. Even a guy who hasn't had one romantic thought in his life will suddenly become creative when expressing his affection. Love makes him want to live a life that produces joy and surprises. Fall in love with something, and you will learn what it takes to keep it going. The same goes for the church. Perhaps instead of having so many planning meetings, we need to have more meetings on how we can express our love.

Years ago my wife responded to a call in the neighborhood about a family who needed food. She went to our food bank, gathered up supplies, and went to the house. It was in an extremely poor neighborhood. When she arrived, she knocked on the apartment door and the mother answered. My wife peeked into the house and saw the children dirty, shoeless, and poor. She saw mattresses lying everywhere. She wasn't ready for what was about to happen next.

She walked in with basic food and raw zucchini, and the children ran up to her, grabbed the bag from her hand, and started gnawing on raw zucchini. The experience was so troubling that afterward Caroline stopped her car on the side of the road and began to cry.

On her way home she saw a box truck, similar to an ice cream truck. She visualized that truck being used as a mobile food bank. Over time she raised enough money for one truck, then two trucks, then three, and on and on. Now eight trucks are going to thirty sites a week distributing food.

Love finds a way! Love opens the door to dreams that could never come across our minds without it. Love is the greatest factory of ideas. My prayer used to be, "God, teach me how to be creative." Now I pray, "God, teach me how to love."

The Bible says, "For God so loved the world, that he gave his only begotten Son, that whosoever believeth in him should not perish, but have everlasting life" (John 3:16 KJV). God gave us this glorious plan of salvation. The most creative, innovative solution of all time: Jesus giving His life as a substitute for man's sins. God loved the world, and then He gave. His plan was generated by love.

■

A group of people in our church started an outreach at a Laundromat. The idea was simple: show up with a row of quarters and put quarters in the machines of the people who need money for their laundry. Who would ever believe a roll of quarters could spark such joy? People were saying things like,

"Because you paid for the laundry we now can buy food." A little revival broke out in that Laundromat.

Compassion opens the door for people to come to Christ. I'm convinced of it. Jesus fed the people before He ministered to them. Evangelism and serving go hand in hand. People often have to be drawn to what they see in you first before they are drawn to the Savior.

Hundreds of people accept Christ weekly at our church, and in almost every case they came to know Christ because someone did something during the week that drew them into the church. Someone loved them, built a relationship with them, fixed something in their house. There's no difference between social gospel and spiritual gospel: it's simply representing Jesus the right way.

Jesus had so much love for people that they couldn't figure Him out. He healed on the Sabbath, He fed people, and He forgave "unforgivable" sins. His grace shocked culture. It didn't fit in. His love was a revolutionary love. Love caused Him to do things no one would ever think of. It took Him to places others would not go—even to the cross.

I think that in our social-media-crazed world, people are bigger targets for ridicule. A person says something wrong, and within seconds the world will hear about it. A politician fails, and all of a sudden they will get hundreds of responses by way of Twitter or Facebook or, worse still, the nightly news. I wonder how Jesus would respond.

I'm sure He would come to the rescue of the fallen a lot

more than we do. We often pick the areas where we want to forgive but stay quiet about other areas. Many people get irate with others who sin differently than they do. When we pick and choose what we want to restore, that's not really grace. It's selective grace.

Here's what I've learned. People who make lists of what sins are worse than others rarely have their own sins in the top ten. Misfit love is not afraid to take a stance of restoration that is unpopular. Love has one great goal, and that is to obliterate shame.

I've been a pastor for twenty years, and I've had the honor of working with all kinds of people going through every type of recovery you can probably think of. Working with hundreds living in our facility daily, I have come to learn the single most destructive force on the comeback road to freedom is *shame*.

So I'm on a mission to obliterate shame!

Let me give you a simple formula:

SHAME = GIVING UP

Shame seeks to first crush and then throw away the broken pieces. I believe shame produces nothing, creates nothing, and leads to nothing. When someone loses hope, however, and some crazy second-chance person comes onto the scene, things start to change. The best thing we can do when someone fails is to run to him or her and infuse hope to a ridiculous level, to the point he or she can see a sunlit future again. If people have hope, then there's a reason to repent. And repentance leads to freedom.

Many could criticize and ask, "Where is the accountability?" My question in return is, "Where is the responsibility we have before God to pick these people back up?" Accountability will come once a person is on his or her feet, but the first step in helping people toward a comeback is a massive infusion of love that brings hope.

Hope produces momentum for people to want to change because they finally have the wind to their backs. Natural accountability will ride on the back of unconditional love. The Bible says, "Where there is no revelation, people cast off restraint" (Prov. 29:18). This means, if there is no hope for the future, there is no hope for self-control. Why even try? We must throw bombs of hope on people right when they fail, to remind them life is not over.

At the Dream Center, more than 70 percent of my staff are graduates from our recovery home. As mentioned before, we have ex-pimps, prostitutes, murderers, and gang members—and that's just the pastoral staff. I feel my job is to throw buckets of grace on people every day, because it's the only way people can make it! After all, how in the world is telling a twenty-year heroin addict "you should be ashamed of yourself" going to create any change? Those reactions simply send people back to the cold, dark alleys for another hit.

God hasn't called us to point out the obvious, that people have sinned (I'm pretty sure they know it), but to show them a bright future they never dreamed possible. I would rather stand before God and hear Him say, "You were too forgiving," than to simply give up and miss all the angels unaware, waiting in the form of hurting people.

I am proud to be part of a ministry that destroys shame and raises up a generation of wounded warriors who become city janitors, walking through the streets of our cities, picking up broken pieces, and telling people they can dream again.

We shouldn't have to explain why we love others; we should just keep on doing it. We can all say, "Jesus loved me despite my failures, and I have no reason why I can't live in extravagant grace." I know I sometimes question spontaneous acts of love and wonder if it's God or not. I've talked myself out of compassion way too many times. But when I do respond in love, joy always seems to follow.

I was flying home from a conference in Buffalo, New York, and I had to stop in the Atlanta airport to make my flight connection to Los Angeles. I was exhausted, and to tell you the truth, I needed a hug. I was tired of airplanes, tired of raising money for the Dream Center, and I just wanted to be home in my bed. Walking around airports isn't my idea of fun, but a glimmer of hope shone in the distance: the Dunkin' Donuts sign.

Standing in the long line looking at the menu, I began to think and pray. *God, why is my attitude so bad? Help me get out of this.* Then the Lord impressed upon me a powerful idea: *Serve through your burden.* Trying to figure out how to do that in a

Dunkin' Donuts line was not easy. Then I heard the voice behind me of a woman who was looking at the menu and talking to her husband. She said, "It's been so long since I've had a donut. I sure would like to have one of those sour-cream donuts."

I turned around. She was a classy-looking lady probably in her fifties. She did not look like the kind of lady who would want a donut. She kept talking about wanting one but didn't get in line. I turned around and asked, "Why don't you get one?" She hesitated and said, "I probably shouldn't get one."

Then I realized she was doing what my wife does. My wife believes that as long as you agonize over the calories, they don't count against you. And if someone buys it for you, the calories pass on to the one who is transferring the food. I said, "I'll buy you the donut and I'll pass it to you, and therefore the calories don't count on you." She laughed.

I drew a big line with my hand in the form of a circle and said, "Do you know where you are standing? You are standing in the no-judgment zone." When she first got the donut, she nibbled on it like a reluctant squirrel. Then after tasting how heavenly it was, she ate that donut quicker than Cookie Monster, and enjoyed it even more. It was such a small gesture of love, but it was enough to pull me out of myself and into someone else's world.

When you put yourself in someone else's world, you tend to forget about your own problems, struggles, and heartaches. There is nothing more beautiful than fighting selfishness with love. Nothing more incredible than making someone else's day great even though yours might feel subpar. The great cure for a bad day is to help someone else have a great one.

■

One of the single mothers who lives at the Dream Center wanted to take me out to the same streets of Hollywood she used to roam. Anatasha is one of those amazing young ladies whose lives are being turned around at the Dream Center. She would be considered what Hollywood calls one of the "children of the night."

Most homeless teens who roam the streets of Hollywood were either runaway teenagers, emancipated minors, or kicked out of their homes. They end up on Hollywood Boulevard, the "boulevard of broken dreams." It's incredible to see the concrete stars on the street with the famous names of celebrities and know that just behind those streets live runaway youths. Every time I see these homeless teens I say to myself, *These are somebody's babies.* The greater sadness is when I ask myself, *Does anybody really care?*

Anatasha survived the streets of Hollywood and is flourishing at the Dream Center. Here is her story.

My name is Anatasha. I'm twenty-six, and I'm from Los Angeles, California. I grew up in Hollywood and I lived with my grandmother, my mom, and my uncle in some apartments. My mom was pretty young when she had me and was always out partying, so my grandma mostly took care of me.

One day my mom left and she never came back. So we moved out of the apartments where we were living and went to Glendale. It was just me and my grandma living together, but then my grandmother found her baby she gave away for adoption, my aunt, and it was like a family reunion.

I started staying with my aunt in Ohio. After about seven or eight years, my aunt got in touch with my mom again, and my mom offered to let me live with her. So I moved in with my mom.

Our family is very dysfunctional. I've never been verbally abused or physically abused, but it's still dysfunctional. Now that I'm older, I know what was going on. My mom was a drug dealer and my father was a gangbanger. The last time I saw him was when I was a baby, and then he ended up going to jail for life. I don't know if he is dead or alive.

The most random things would happen when I was growing up in my mom's house, like the house would get raided or I would walk in on my mom shooting up heroin. Eventually my mom sent me back to Ohio, and I bounced back and forth. I ended up in court because my aunt was fighting for me, my grandma was fighting for me, and my mom was fighting for me, but I ultimately chose my mom.

Three months later my mom put me in foster care, because she said she couldn't handle anything and had to get rid of me and my sisters. She told us she would come pick me up in three months from wherever I would be, but I didn't see her until eight years later. She recently popped up in my life, but this time she was clean and sober, and she made up for the years she spent away. Three months after that she passed away.

I was twelve when they put me in foster care the first time. I would beat up the other kids because I was really angry at what happened, and I started drinking. I was scared for my sisters, and I couldn't find my grandma because my mom had isolated me from the rest of my family. The foster-care agency was looking for them too.

Now that I'm a mom, I never want my children to experience that feeling. The way my mom treated me made me realize I need to step up more and make sure my children never ever lose me, no matter what situation I'm in. I may not be able to give them everything they want, but I know the one thing they really need, because I needed it: love from their mother.

I haven't done a real good job. I have been selfish, and I continued using drugs even after I had my kids. I continued partying and making wrong decisions, but I'm able to say now that I have stepped up. Better late than never.

I just got my GED at the Dream Center. When I first

came here I was at a third-grade level in everything, but I got my GED in two months. I ended up scoring a 590 on my test, which is pretty good. That made me feel so good—that I was smart, and I wasn't as dumb as people said I was.

I want to study to become a social worker, so I'm going to get my associate's degree in psychology and work up from there. My daughter told me she was proud of me when she found out I passed my GED. Everyone said that, but when my eight-year-old daughter said it, it was all I needed to hear. It shows her I'm trying.

I have known about the Dream Center for a long time. I used to work at a KFC and Taco Bell nearby, and one night a whole bunch of Dream Center people came in. They looked so happy that I asked them what the Dream Center was for, and they said they provided help for everything. So I came down and started getting what I needed.

One day I saw a family come out of the building, and they looked so happy and secure. The father of my children had started to become abusive, and I had gotten heavier into drugs. I had hit my rock bottom, and I knew I needed to change. If the only thing I could depend on was the man who was beating me every day, then I knew I had nothing to lose.

So I called the Dream Center and had an over-the-phone interview. It seemed impossible for me to get in at first, but three weeks later they called to explain the rules and they said they would see me the next day. But I came that night. If it wasn't for the Dream Center or the family floor, I would probably be in the same house with the father of my kids. I would be hooked on drugs and partying, and I wouldn't even be stable enough to take care of my kids.

Anatasha took me back to her new outreach site. That's right! She now pastors one of the blocks around the Dream Center. The night she took me out, I met runaway kids from as far away as Ohio. I wanted to find out how these "children of the night" get to this city, so I asked one of the young runaway girls who was nineteen how she ended up in Hollywood. Her answer astonished me. She said, "Because it's safer on the dangerous streets of Hollywood than in the home I was raised in, in Ohio."

Anatasha took us further down the Hollywood track. Teenagers were suffering the pain the lack of love causes. The encouraging part was watching a girl like Anatasha, once labeled a misfit, helping others. Usually when someone overcomes impossible odds, it's because someone loved them in a way that seems radical, genuine, and out of the box.

■

One day after a service I was standing at the back door shaking hands with people as they exited. A man came up to me and thanked me for the sermon. We were close to Christmas and jokingly I asked him what he wanted for Christmas. It was a trivial question—more of a conversation starter than anything else. He looked at me with great sadness and said, "A second chance."

Never breaking stride, he continued down the sidewalk heading out to the church parking lot. I thought about the scripture found in Proverbs 24:16: "For though the righteous fall seven times, they rise again, but the wicked stumble when calamity strikes."

A just man falls seven times but gets back up. Oftentimes people can't get up by themselves, and they need to be shown misfit love before they will have the strength to rise again. How many people feel that life is over after devastation? When a person falls, they want to get up, but the reality is they need someone to help them up. I haven't seen that man in years but his Christmas request reminds me of the longing of so many. I wonder what their lives could become if someone just offered them each a second chance.

People wanting to turn a corner often need a bridge. Our love is the bridge that can help them get to their permanent destination—the cross. I've seen people come out of twenty-year addictions, break the cycle of prison, and be the first in their families to go to college. Every single time there's a story of someone who believed in them, took a chance, and gave them a second chance at life. Misfit love at work.

ten

MISFIT OBEDIENCE

When you respond to the call of God in obedience, be ready to be misunderstood. Also be ready to be labeled irresponsible.

Abraham responded when God told him to go to a land he had never seen before. Noah built an ark back when no one knew what an ark was. David picked up a rock to sling it at an armed giant. I hope one day in heaven we'll be able to roll back the audiotape and hear the conversations these men had before they stepped out in faith. I'm sure it would be fascinating to hear phrases like, "You are just too optimistic" or "Come back to reality" or "Why don't you do something more in line with your ability?"

Expressions of doubt can be confirmation you are on the right track. Obedience is often so difficult. When we bought the Dream Center, it seemed that we cried every night because the task of renovating this hospital was just too big.

When you drive by the Dream Center while heading down

the Hollywood Freeway, you'll see how our building hovers over the skyline and is more visible than probably any building from downtown to Hollywood. Trying to run this hospital, we were so broke that many nights I would get off the freeway just to turn off a light in the building that should not have been on in the middle of the night. Things were that tough.

Obedience doesn't guarantee you won't question yourself. It just guarantees that if you hang in there long enough, you will see the reward. The blessing will come when you need it the most. We often reap blessings that are consequences of acts of obedience years ago. Scripture urges us: "Let us not become weary in doing good, for at the proper time we will reap a harvest if we do not give up" (Gal. 6:9). There are some blessings that only come about by simple obedience. Even if it sounds crazy.

We have another great Dream Center in New York City. The pastor's name is Brad Reed. He pastors a fantastic church in the heart of the city. His road to the Big Apple began in a small community in Alabama. One night Brad was watching Christian television, and they were doing a special feature on the Dream Center. Brad felt God speak to him to get on a Greyhound bus the next day and come visit us at the Dream Center in LA, where he believed God would make him into a disciple of Christ's.

He got himself a bus ticket and made the several-day journey from his small town in Alabama to Los Angeles. When he arrived at the campus, the contrast between LA and his small Alabama town could not have been greater. With his thick Alabama accent, he said, "I want to be a disciple" to the first guy he saw on the Dream Center campus. The guy said, "You do?" He said, "Yes."

Brad was thinking maybe he would be put in our internship program, or a Bible school type program. He didn't realize that our rehab program is called discipleship. When he asked to be a disciple, he was telling us he wanted to be in the one-year, live-in recovery home. The man said, "All right, then."

Brad's attitude was incredible. After a few days, he realized he was in the wrong program. He shared a room with people who were coming off drugs. Some of the folks were having seizures. This was not what he had in mind. It wasn't in the brochure.

But here's the amazing thing about Brad. He never asked to be transferred. After all, he'd asked to be a disciple. Why not stay in this program for a year? Simple obedience led him to a place he wasn't expecting, but God wanted him there. Flourishing in the program, he became a leader and excelled in everything he did.

After graduating the program he would later marry the youth pastor, and together they would lead the youth ministry at the church. Little did he realize that years later he would be the pastor of the New York Dream Center. Every bit of experience he obtained while living in a rehab program would turn out to be the training he would need to be a pastor.

The reward in obedience usually comes by sticking it out.

Obedience opens the door for endless possibilities. Refuse to listen to any voice that tells you instant results are confirmations you are on the right track. The road might be longer than you expected, but that does not mean you are off the right path. Misfit obedience might not make a lot of sense in the short term, but in the long term it proves itself right.

■

It's amazing to see people at the Dream Center who are one good decision or one bad decision away from finding or losing their lives. Their futures pivot on choices of obedience or disobedience—maybe on choosing to forgive someone who greatly hurt them or choosing to leave a certain comfort zone. These acts of obedience might seem difficult, but one day they'll realize the tough thing to do was the right thing to do.

It's a beautiful thing when you see people respond the right way, surrender, and break the chains of bad decisions. People like Isabella. Here's her story.

I grew up in a Catholic family with three brothers and a sister. I was born in Mexico and came to the US when I was three years old. My parents were poor, but we never went hungry. My early childhood was beautiful. I was Daddy's little girl, and I felt very loved.

When I turned about twelve years of age, I remember my father starting to distance himself from me, and

I could not really understand why. Looking back, it was probably awkward for my dad that his "little girl" was not little anymore.

Around that same time, my mother had to find work outside of the home because things were getting harder financially. My older brother and I became the heads of the household at home, and that was the end of my beautiful childhood.

I really don't know if my older brother had already been introduced to drugs at that time, but my guess is he had. A family had moved in next door to us, who I later found out were part of a Mexican drug cartel. These people were drug lords, but I was much too young and innocent to understand any of that.

What I do remember, however, is that my older brother became a violent monster. Not only was he verbally abusive, but he was also physically abusive. He used to beat up all of us. I couldn't bear it when he would hit my younger siblings, so I would get in the middle and I eventually became his punching bag. At first I would fight back, as he wasn't that much bigger than me. But as he got older and bigger, I was no match for his strength.

When my parents would come home, I would tell them about the fighting, but they never took it seriously, usually putting it off as not being a big deal. They would make comments such as, "You probably did something to deserve it" or "You're exaggerating." No matter what, my parents never dealt with the problem, so it got worse.

By this time, my brother was also being very open about his drug and alcohol consumption, and he had quit school. Things were getting worse at home, and my mom and dad didn't seem to know how to handle my older brother's out-of-control behavior.

As much as I tried to stay away from drugs and alcohol, I eventually caved when I was around sixteen. I had been invited to a wedding shower for a coworker, but I ended up going to another party to see a guy I liked. He was much older than I was, and not only was he good-looking, but he told me he liked me. I felt somewhat safe with him. When I got to the party, this guy became very aggressive with me and ended up forcing me to drink. He then he took me away and raped me.

That was the day I spiritually died. Up until that time, I believed there was a God watching over me who would not allow this kind of evil in my life. I got away from this man three different times before he raped me that night, and each time I thanked God for saving me. But this guy was faster and stronger than I was, and eventually he took me to an empty park in Glendale, California, and brutally raped me.

Even though this guy eventually let me go, I just wanted to die. How could I go home looking like this?

What would I tell my parents? So I decided I was going to kill myself. I was already dead inside anyhow. I was no longer a virgin. After that, I no longer cared about myself.

I began drinking at first, and then eventually when the alcohol could not numb me enough from the emotional pain, I began using harder drugs. Nothing took away the pain. The rape was pretty much swept under the rug, because it was shameful in my culture. It was never confronted or dealt with.

My older brother's physical abusiveness continued well into my high school years, and I felt unloved and unprotected. I had met a wonderful young man who loved me dearly, but I drove him away, maybe because I didn't know how to be loved. I went from bad relationship to bad relationship and ended up each time more alone and depressed. I learned to hide it, and I graduated from high school.

After I graduated, all I wanted to do was move out of my abusive home, so I worked hard to save up. College was not important—I just needed to get out of that house. I became resentful toward my parents and did not feel they cared about me. One of my brothers and I both decided we would work and put our resources together to move out.

We told our parents what we planned on doing, and our abusive brother overheard. He told my mom that we wouldn't be moving out, because he was not going to be living there much longer. He was right. He was killed in a motorcycle accident shortly after that conversation. It was painful, but at the same time, the family was relieved.

That time of my life became even more confusing, as people around me were telling me I should be glad that my abuser was dead. But he was my brother, and no matter what, I still loved him!

I got deeper into drugs and alcohol, and my depression turned into fits of anger. I was now on a suicide mission. I also was working at a law firm and had just been promoted to mailroom supervisor when my brother died. Shortly thereafter, I met a guy I would eventually become engaged to. His family was into Santeria—a combination of West African religions and Roman Catholicism—and I was ignorant to the consequences of that lifestyle.

He also got me pregnant. But before I found out, I broke off the engagement. Because I didn't want any connection with the man or his family, I made an immediate decision to abort my baby. Again, I had no idea what kind of consequences there would be for my poor choices.

More drugs, more alcohol, and more men came into my life. I did not want to think or feel. I was making more money, and I partied every chance I got. I also bought a brand-new car and I was so proud of myself! But because of my party lifestyle, one night as I was coming home from a club, I passed out behind the wheel and I drove my brand-new car into a brick wall. I was not wearing my seat belt.

The injuries I sustained were so severe that I had an out-of-body experience. When I realized I had been in a car wreck and that I wasn't having some bad dream, I began to thank God my sorry life was finally going to be over and I was finally going to stop hurting. I had faked every day of my life up until that point and I was tired of faking it.

I let out a sigh and felt myself drifting upward. I could see myself in the car, and what I felt was the best feeling I had ever felt. It was relief. I don't remember how much time had gone by, but I suddenly saw my parents mourning my brother's death. As I saw their pain, I realized they were going to have to now mourn my death.

At that very moment, I began begging God to not let me die. I didn't want to put my parents through more pain. (I would have been the third child they would have lost. I had another brother who died when he was only ten months old.)

After I prayed that God not take me home, I was instantly back in my body. There were paramedics at the scene, and I was taken to a hospital. I did not know the extent of my injuries, and while I was glad to be alive, it was not going to be long before I would regret surviving that car wreck.

For almost fifteen years, I underwent multiple surgeries and had chronic pain that left me more depressed and addicted to prescription medication. I also developed severe endometriosis, which left me with the inability to have children. The chronic pain was diagnosed as fibromyalgia, and as the years passed, I became more crippled. I was frequently on disability, and I found it very hard to stay employed.

I was working in a law firm not far from the Dream Center, and it was at that time a coworker introduced me to meth. He made it sound like it was just what I needed to deal with that hellish job, so I took my first hit and was instantly hooked.

In just a few years, everything I had worked for was gone. I began to plan my suicide. But one night, as I was lying down in a near-catatonic state, I heard a song on TV that snapped me out of it and into a revelation. I felt the presence of what could have been angelic hosts, and I knew in my heart that suicide was not the way. That night I made a promise to God that I would no longer consider suicide. I thought things were going to get better, but they did not.

During the summer the sheriff's department came and escorted me out of my apartment. I was being evicted. My family was ashamed of me. My father was also dying from cancer, and my family didn't want me near him. I didn't want to tell my dad I was homeless, but he knew my life was falling apart and my siblings were not willing to help me. That broke his heart. He died that fall.

My family left me behind on the way to my father's funeral. Two of my longtime friends went looking for me and picked me up so I could be there. After he was buried, my family turned their backs on me and did not want anything to do with me.

The day of the funeral, I lost my entire family. Shortly thereafter, my friends no longer wanted anything to do with me either—even those who had been in my life more than fifteen years. I was truly alone and heavily addicted to a drug that numbed all my pain.

I was living in a metal toolshed when all this took place. The police came and took me out of that toolshed and I had nowhere else to go. I still had a car that belonged to the bank. For some reason I did not qualify for welfare benefits, so I survived off recycling money.

One day I was too sick to pick up any more cans and bottles, and my heart was too broken to care anymore. I was angry with God, not understanding why He would allow me to go through all this. I had no more strength or will left in me, so I was going to sit underneath a tree at the park and wait to die.

I was sick, tired, and hungry, and if that did not kill me, then I knew I would soon die from a broken heart. I began to cry out to God in agony, begging Him to take my life, when I began to feel a warm presence come over me. I felt something lift me, and I was led into the bathroom of the park.

What I experienced in that park bathroom that night can only be explained as a divine encounter with my heavenly Father. As I looked at myself in the aluminum mirror, I could hear a gentle voice telling me everything was going to be okay. I responded with "I know," because I suddenly felt overwhelming peace fill me.

Then I heard the words *I love you*, and I felt a surge of love overwhelm me. I nodded in agreement because I felt loved for the very first time in my life. My right hand then wiped the tears from my face, but it didn't feel like it was my hand. Then I heard those words again—*I love you*—and I replied, "I know," because I felt another surge of love.

Then my hand began to caress my hair, again not feeling like my hand, but instead, the hand of a loving being that I could not see. I knew it was God. I heard *I love you* for the third time and I knew I was going to come out of this mess of a life. I didn't know how, but I knew that I was going to be okay.

Many miracles would take place after that day that

would eventually lead me to the Dream Center almost four years later. Those miracles would prepare me for so many things that I would experience here.

I was involved in a burglary (which I thought was a drug pickup) where the book *The Purpose Driven Life* was stolen. That book was going to answer many questions I had about God and my life.

I learned to survive. I ate out of trash cans and slept on rooftops, sometimes in the park. There were many times when I trusted the wrong people and was sexually abused and even locked in their houses. At one point I became a state's witness against criminals who tried to stop me from testifying by putting a contract out on my life. I got away from them each time.

I gave up my spirit to the Lord many times, thinking I was going to be killed. By that time, I knew I would be going home to Jesus, but I was not going without a fight. I actually wanted to live and not die!

In the midst of running from my enemies, I realized I had been told many years before, after my accident, that I would never run again. I had been healed and did not even realize it! When my car was impounded, all my medication was in the car. That was God's plan to get me off my meds!

My addiction to meth continued until twenty-six days before I would come to the Dream Center. I have not touched meth since then. My family has been

restored, and many of my family members are coming
to the Lord!

The common thread behind every one of these amazing
stories is people crying out to God and then moving forward
in obedience. Crossroads moments in our lives are monu-
mental. We can often feel the assurance of God wanting us to
move; the hard thing is being willing to make the first move.
Simple obedience can send our lives on an adventure that is so
powerful we may end up living lives we never knew possible.

This story clearly indicates that it's never too late to make a
good decision. We are humans. We make mistakes. The beautiful thing is that even when we miss our moments of obedience,
God still gives other chances to make positive decisions.

The misconception is that when we miss our chances to
be obedient, we never get second chances. This is simply not
true. The mercy and grace of God will always present another
chance to get it right and do it God's way. There's a reason
the Bible speaks of mercy being renewed morning by morning
(Lam. 3:22–23).

Many days in my life, I've felt that I had missed my chance
to respond in obedience to Christ in one situation or another.
But I've chosen not to live in regret. I'll just keep my ear
inclined to the next moment of surrender that presents itself.
There's too much life left to live to beat ourselves up regarding
yesterday's failures. God's mercy is so powerful that even if we
throw in the towel, God will always give us another one.

Life doesn't end at disobedience. There's always a way to turn it around, even after years of disobedience. You might have missed some moments in the past, but you don't have to miss the moments in front of you. As long as you have a pulse, God still has a plan. There's no such thing as "three strikes and you're out" in the kingdom of God. You always have a chance to make a powerful decision regarding your future.

■

I recently had the wonderful privilege of doing a wedding in Rome. A couple in our church flew me out to perform the ceremony in a gorgeous Episcopal church. That week in Rome, I must have walked six or seven miles a day. The only time I would stop would be to devour pasta every couple of miles. Seven miles wasn't long enough to burn off the calories I consumed.

In between eating and walking and sightseeing, I came across a church in a small community. Walking around mid-morning, I saw two or three people in the church praying. I sat in the back of that chapel, and all of a sudden, seeing those people pray brought a huge feeling of regret back into my spirit.

Ten years ago, I felt strongly that the Dream Center needed a place of prayer to be open every day for twenty-four straight hours. A place that would become a beacon of hope to the community. Imagine someone being there all hours of the day to help people in dire situations who needed prayer.

Regret flooded my soul because this was something I

should have started years ago, and I had clearly been disobedient. Sitting in the back row of that church and seeing the people having a place to pray reminded me of what I knew I should have done years before. Leaving the chapel, I walked down the road, tears rolled down my face, and I cried out to God, "Forgive me!"

A ray of light peeked out from the clouds. I'm not sure that ray was just for me, but it was enough to symbolize a new beginning. Seeing the sun spark behind the clouds was a reminder that there are still bright lights behind the clouds of our lives. Ten years later, the twenty-four-hour prayer center is in full operation. It took me a while to get to that place of obedience, but we arrived. Every day the chapel is occupied with incredible numbers of people seeking the beautiful face of our second-chance God.

Reflecting on yesterday's disobedience will take us nowhere. Today is the day, now is the time to rekindle a life of openness and obedience. The life of Peter is a beautiful expression of obedience, disobedience, and coming back to obedience. Peter had the courage to follow Jesus at the simple request of, "Come, follow me."

As Jesus was walking beside the Sea of Galilee, he saw two brothers, Simon called Peter and his brother Andrew. They were casting a net into the lake, for they were fishermen.

"Come, follow me," Jesus said, "and I will send you out to fish for people." At once they left their nets and followed him. (Matt. 4:18–20)

That was incredible obedience on the part of Peter and Andrew, who responded "at once" to this man named Jesus. Peter's obedience to the request of Jesus opened the door for him to be a disciple and go on a life-changing journey. But later Peter would become disobedient. After Jesus died on the cross, Peter joined the others as they scattered in fear.

> Then the slave-girl who kept the door said to Peter, "You are not also one of this man's disciples, are you?"
> He said, "I am not." (John 18:17 NASB)

Peter's initial obedience sent him on a journey with Jesus that was full of awe and wonder. But later by the fire, denying he even knew Jesus sent Peter on a totally different road that led him to shame and a lack of belief. Peter went from obedience to disobedience. The great thing about this story is that Jesus gave him a chance to be obedient again.

After the resurrection, Jesus visited Peter again along the seashore. He had gone back to being a fisherman. Some think Peter was in a backslidden place, giving up on his calling, back to his old occupation.

> "I'm going out to fish," Simon Peter told them, and they said, "We'll go with you." So they went out and got into the boat, but that night they caught nothing.
> Early in the morning, Jesus stood on the shore, but the disciples did not realize that it was Jesus.

He called out to them, "Friends, haven't you any fish?"

"No," they answered.

He said, "Throw your net on the right side of the boat and you will find some." When they did, they were unable to haul the net in because of the large number of fish.

Then the disciple whom Jesus loved said to Peter, "It is the Lord!" As soon as Simon Peter heard him say, "It is the Lord," he wrapped his outer garment around him (for he had taken it off) and jumped into the water. (John 21:3–7)

I love Peter's enthusiasm. There's nothing more joyful for a father than when he comes home and his children run and jump into his arms. This is what Peter was doing. Peter was so excited to see Jesus that he couldn't wait for the boat to dock. Peter knew that to see Jesus again was to see grace. His leaping off the boat was a sign that Peter would renew himself back to obedience.

Jesus had a long talk with Peter by the campfire about the road he was about to take. Peter would make the most of this opportunity and become a disciple with depth and maturity.

There is life after giving up. There is life after throwing in the towel. For every act of disobedience that sends us down a miserable path, another act of surrender can send us down a great one. The quicker we get back up from falling, the more time we will have to redeem for success. Anyone who embraces obedience will find that life is never over at the point of crushing defeat. We have a God who gives us another shot at obedience.

Take it!

eleven

MISFITS AND MESSY MINISTRY

After spending a week at the Dream Center, a person described it perfectly to me: "This place is organized chaos." Chaos is a gift to the person who thinks everything must fit perfectly, because chaos is where Jesus shows up.

We must meet people in their chaos before we lead them to Christ. Jesus knew there were miracles under the rubble; that's why He went to the places others would not go. He had dinner with tax collectors. He was known as a friend of sinners. He associated with a woman caught in the act of adultery. His first disciples were rugged fishermen. No environment was too messy for Jesus' ministry.

One day a homeless family came to church needing a place to stay. It was an urgent situation for this large family—an issue of survival. Here's the problem: these people were disrupting my perfect timeline. Helping homeless families was still two years down the road in my master plan for the program. I had not yet learned to stay flexible enough to adapt to chaos.

A young lady in our church named Kelli Bradley was also preparing for the launch of our family floor two years down the road. The family begged for a place to stay. The thought of a family of seven living in a car just broke my heart.

I called Kelli over and said, "It's time to start the family floor."

Kelli said, "Great," thinking it would be two years down the road before the door actually opened.

I said, "How about today?" Praise God for people in life who embrace chaos right alongside of you. "Kelli, can we take in this family right now?"

She said, "Let's go for it."

I promised her that we would keep this quiet, and this would be the only family we would take in.

To my total surprise, not long after, the staff opened up an entire hospital floor with twenty-six rooms for families to live in. When they showed me the new place, I was in total disbelief they had made it happen so quickly, in just one week. I told them, "I only said one family!"

Kelli responded with a laugh. "Pastor, once we took in one family we knew you would never stop, so we prepared all these rooms in advance."

Blessed are the flexible, for they shall be bent but not broken.

God often sends people into your life with a single need that could open the door to so much more. We don't wait for money to come before we start a program; we wait for the encounter with chaos. We never know the full plan until we jump in. Faith is just that—taking the leap.

The Bible describes it this way: "Now faith is confidence in what we hope for and assurance about what we do not see" (Heb. 11:1). If we can see the solution and the way to do something, it's not faith; it's human power. If you want to give yourself the glory, you do what only you can do. If you want to give God the glory, you do what you can't do.

Misfits in God's work are not afraid to jump into the mud. When someone needs a ride home, we don't try to find a way to pass the assignment on to someone else. We make ourselves available.

I used to play Pop Warner football when I was a kid. I was the skinniest kid on the team. In fact, I was so skinny that when I stuck out my tongue I looked like a zipper. All season long I got hit, and hit hard. Frustrated, I told my dad I was tired of getting hit every game, and I felt like a punching bag.

My dad taught me a lesson that went beyond football. He said, "The best way not to get hurt is to jump into the pile. You're getting hurt because you just stand around. Next time there's a pile, just jump in." It was great advice. I changed my attitude from timid to tenacious.

Life is too short to play it safe. Jump into the chaos. Misfits embrace messy ministry. I'm not talking about church life or pastoral ministry, but a lifestyle that says, "I'm not afraid to respond when I have the power to do so."

The rush, the adrenaline, the joy we can get from jumping in to solve a problem in chaos can literally be addicting. I learned this on a ranch from a hero of mine—a pastor named

Willie George. He is the ultimate outdoorsman. When he invited me to go hunting with him, my first response was, "That's the last thing I want to do. I'm a city boy. I've never been hunting in my entire life, and the idea of walking around in freezing cold weather doesn't get me excited."

But Willie convinced me that a few days in God's open country would be good to clear the mind, so we set off on a buck-hunting adventure. Before we left, his assistant gave me a quick tutorial about shooting a gun. "You need to breathe easy, because when you see a buck you will get buck fever." The sight of a buck in your scope can cause the moment to overwhelm you.

He said, "Some people will miss their moment when the time comes because they can actually freeze up when the moment arrives to pull the trigger. Many have missed their trophy buck because, in the chaos of the moment, they missed their shot."

I thought about that comment all week long. It's such a shame to miss your moment because you're afraid to pull the trigger. You could have a hand in the destiny of someone's life, and yet you hold back love because you're afraid to respond in the moment. The truth is, many of us love people but are afraid to pull the trigger when the moment arrives.

Afraid of what sacrifice that moment can lead to.

Afraid of rejection if we share our faith.

Afraid of the cost.

Afraid that our comfort zone will be interrupted by the needs of others.

We have the power to make a difference, but are we willing to pull the trigger?

This letter was recently published in our monthly newsletter:

A few weeks ago, I was approached on the street corner by a woman with a flyer. I quickly noticed that a meal was offered along with bus transportation to and from the Dream Center church later that evening. Like most every day, I had spent all my money on crack cocaine earlier that morning and was feeling guilty, lonely, and very, very, hungry.

I recently came from the Midwest, where my addiction took priority over my family, home, job, and self-respect, to the point that I ate from a Dumpster on Easter Sunday, in the same town where my family lived.

I came west hoping and praying to overcome my chronic use of crack. Within a few days of arriving in Los Angeles, I was smoking crack once again. I came to the conclusion that I would continue using and most likely die on the streets of Skid Row. I felt relieved that at least I wouldn't put my family through any more grief, since they had seen me in countless rehabs, jails, and hospitals.

When the lady handed me the flyer that day, I must confess I was interested only in the meal. The service seemed to last forever. *How long is this guy going to speak?* I was thinking. *Yeah, yeah, get to the point. I'm hungry!* Well, something must have got through to me that night. Through prayer and faith, I remained clean for a day, then for a couple of days. Then a week.

I found myself back at the Dream Center. This time I enjoyed the music and listened to your message. That was weeks and weeks ago, and I find myself looking forward to and attending the Sunday service. It goes by way too fast! I've been clean now for the longest time in my life, and have made contact with my family. And God through Jesus has blessed my life in a thousand ways. Thank you!

Signed,

Anonymous

Just an ordinary woman handing out flyers, embracing chaos, led to this person's transformation. One of the reasons we are afraid to embrace chaos is that we think we have to clean ourselves up before we can serve. We think there's some level of holiness we have to obtain before we can help people. We feel like a broken piece, but broken pieces can lead people to refuge.

There's a wonderful story about literal broken pieces in the book of Acts. Paul and 276 others were aboard a ship when suddenly a storm blew up. Because of that storm, the ship crashed near the shore. Those who could swim got to land, and the rest, the Bible says, "escaped all safe to land." They could not swim, they could not make it in on their own, but it says that "some [came in] on boards, and some on broken pieces" (Acts 27:44 KJV).

If those boards could speak, I wonder what they would say. Maybe something like, "I'm just a little broken piece of the ship. What can I do? I used to be a part of the big, beautiful vessel and now I'm broken off. I'm just a board floating around. I'm not what I used to be." All of a sudden, someone who couldn't swim and who was about to drown saw that broken piece of ship and grabbed ahold of it. The little board now had a reason to live after being broken apart. It safely carried the overboard passengers to safety.

A broken piece just existing, just floating, saved passengers' lives. Misfits and broken pieces are what God uses to bring others to shore. In my old neighborhood I used to walk around the liquor stores where the gang members hung out. I used to walk up to them and say things like, "One day you're going to be my youth pastor. One day you're going to be a pastor." It appeared as though I was the comedian of the hour as they laughed at me.

"Pastor, why are you saying such crazy things to gang members?" I was just walking among the mess, trying to find a messenger. There are miracles in the mud. Everyone has the potential to be a Dream Center. Every house can be a Dream Center—a place of hope. Imagine if the homes of God's people became outposts of hope in every community. It's not necessary that we build big Dream Centers or megachurches all over the world, if every church becomes an outpost of compassion and the hands and feet of Jesus on their block.

We must throw the lifeline of the love of Christ everywhere because miracles are everywhere; we just need to keep looking. Our youth pastor was labeled a misfit. His name is Chris Torres. Here is his story.

God has always had His hand on me, even though I didn't grow up in a church or have much to do with Him unless I was praying for Him to get me out of trouble when I had messed up. This is what God has done for me, and really it's a testimony of a complete transformation and the birth of a dream. A dream is something I never had until God got ahold of me.

As I said already, I was not brought up in the church, so I never had the chance to walk away from the faith because it was something I never had. I am from Rio Rancho, New Mexico, and growing up I loved to get into trouble. It didn't matter what form it came in. I always seemed to find my way to the principal's office, and often I was in a lot of trouble at home as well. My mom and dad were both really good people, so I have no fingers to point or anyone to blame for the wrong decisions I made.

When I got into high school, trips to the county jail started to happen on top of the trips to the principal's office. I joined a gang when I was fifteen years old, and I was not doing well in school at all. I started to sell drugs. It wasn't even because I wanted money, but because I wanted the fame and the name that goes along with being a drug dealer. I didn't accomplish this goal until after high school, but this was when I made decisions that started to compound themselves into bigger problems.

I moved out immediately after high school, and it seemed like a good time to go down to Juarez, Mexico, buy drugs, and drink and party in the clubs. On our way back from one of our trips to Juarez, at three in the morning on an old drug highway in New Mexico, we rolled the car I was riding in.

I flew through the windshield, and the car rolled over on top of my legs. Most of the ligaments in my legs were torn. My forehead was split open and I had reconstructive surgery to reduce the size of the scar. I couldn't stand up for about three weeks after the accident. During my recovery, I used the pain as my introduction to a greater and easier way to sell drugs. I was able to then get an on-call doctor to prescribe me anything I wanted, and I started selling pills.

Along with all this I started to rob other drug dealers and became involved in some major criminal activities. I started to stack up charges through different arrests and on top of this became addicted to the pills I was selling. The fun I used to have was not that much fun anymore. I became extremely paranoid of everyone, and was always strung out on drugs.

The cases were piling up, and I was facing four years

in prison for a felony cocaine charge. My life felt like it was spiraling out of control. Then, to add to all of this, two of my so-called friends with whom I was robbing people turned on me and decided to try and rob me with someone else from another neighborhood. They held me at gunpoint and split my head open as they beat me with a gun.

While I was in the hospital, a friend of mine I grew up with came to visit me. His girlfriend at the time was named Leslie—a girl I'd also grown up with. Leslie's mom was a radical Christian and was having a women's group that night, when Leslie, on her way to the hospital, showed up in tears and asked them to start praying for me. This, to my knowledge, was the first time someone actually began to pray for me.

Shortly after I checked out of the hospital I became fed up with life. I had a strong sense of failure and that life was not going to amount to much for me. Then I decided I was going to at least try and get off of drugs. That was the most pressing issue at the moment, so I told my family what was up and checked into a rehab.

Thirty days later I got out and I started working with a man who listened to a Christian radio station all day. As I heard more and more over the radio, I started to ask questions. I became fascinated with what I was hearing, and I wanted to start going to church. So Leslie's mom, Rose, the one who had prayed for me when I was in the hospital, took me with them to church. When the pastor prayed that day, Rose grabbed my hand and I decided to give my life to Jesus as I wept in my seat.

Everything for me changed and I absolutely fell in love with the church. I loved the atmosphere, the friendliness, all the happy people who were around and happy to talk to me and happy to see me. It was like nothing I had ever experienced. I then heard about the Dream Center and loved what they were doing. This was my opportunity.

I wanted to go to school so that I could obtain the credentials to spend my entire life in the church. I signed up to go to the Dream Center Leadership School, which was called the Movement at that time, and I planned to leave New Mexico on August 30, 2011, to move to LA. I had been sober for more than a year, loved God, loved the church, and was moving to LA. Life was sweet. Then the storm hit.

On August 4, 2011, one of my best friends was killed. It totally wrecked me. I started drinking and smoking again. I never went back to the hard stuff, but I most definitely lost control and lost sight of my plans. Looking back, I can see the importance of what Jesus tells us in Matthew 7:24 about being wise and building our foundations on a solid rock.

I realize now that I was worshiping the church atmosphere more than I was worshiping God. I loved the praise I would receive and the loving people, and that was my focus. So when tragedy struck, I folded. But God's grace still got me to the Dream Center.

When I had completed my second year of school and the leadership program, God completely touched my life. I realized during this time that I would spend my life not just working for a church but doing all that I could to be obedient to the Holy Spirit. I loved to work with kids and was going to school in hopes of one day becoming a pastor, but I did not know how I was going to make that happen. That is when my pastor approached me and asked if I would like to pastor the youth of our church.

Since becoming the youth pastor, I have graduated from college with a degree in Christian ministry. I will be ordained soon, and I have never loved my life more than I do today. I've never been able to dream like I can today. I can dream now because I have seen it come true.

God is my solid foundation, and I get the amazing opportunity of being able to shepherd other young kids into a life where they truly realize how much Jesus loves them. I will glorify Him whenever I get the chance. No matter where that is, if I get a stage, a microphone, a letter to write, or a speech to give, God will be glorified.

I have accomplished more than I ever would have thought possible. It's not just a dream to me anymore—it has become a reality, and a complete transformation.

This, like many other stories of people from the Dream Center, shows us how God raises up people in the midst of the chaos. You heard the story of Kenny, our children's pastor, and now the story of Chris, our youth pastor. I never could have predicted that a majority of my staff would have pasts so dark and yet become people of such great light.

God wants His people to speak life in the middle of chaos, like the prophet Ezekiel spoke life in the valley of dry bones (Ezek. 37:4). Many people have been so run-down their entire lives that when someone speaks life in the midst of their chaos, it becomes a voice so loud, so new, so profound and engaging that it changes everything. It tells them they have the ability to dream.

What stops a young man from joining a gang if there's nothing to live for? What stops a kid from becoming a meth addict when there's nothing to live for? A dream gives people a reason to exercise restraint and make good decisions in their lives. Messy ministry proclaims to people that they have a future when all they can see is the past.

■

As a kid, I had one cross-eye. Every day at school I heard about it from the kids. They laughed at me and mocked me, and I hated second grade. To this day I can remember how every Sunday around 6:00 p.m. I would encounter a wave of depression because school was a few hours away. The kids were relentless. Back then there was no awareness of bullying, and there was no relief for me.

Kids also became very creative in their description of my lazy eye. When my father would drop me off at school, he could see the pain in my eyes. He always gave me a two-minute pep talk before he let me out the door, reminding me how special I was. He told me of the night in Iowa when I was born, when a saintly old man came into the hospital and said, "This boy has a unique calling on his life to do something that's never been done before." My dad would tell me about that prophecy and send me off every day with a fresh dose of love.

He would not let me leave that car until I felt ten feet tall. The best way to describe it is that my father was giving me the "spiritual antibiotics" to be able to handle the assault that was about to hit me. His words sustained me and healed me, as he continued to speak life into my mess, my frailties, and my sadness. God uses people like you and me to walk right into people's messes and speak love and healing.

The Dream Center is often labeled as a place that will take people "at the bottom of the barrel." "They are a ragtag army with misfits." Those comments used to bother me because these people are so much more than that. Then I realized to be labeled a misfit for not being afraid of messy ministry was a compliment.

Have you seen the movie *Moneyball* with Brad Pitt? It's the story about Billy Beane, the owner of the Oakland Athletics baseball team. Every year Billy has to compete with other major-league ball clubs with a budget that's often 20 percent of what other teams spend. The shocking thing is, he always finds a way to win. His teams are always competitive against the flashy, big-market teams like the New York Yankees, Boston Red Sox, and Los Angeles Dodgers.

He's known for scraping the bottom of the barrel and finding diamonds in the rough. Maybe it's a player who has an injury and who others gave up on. Maybe it's an old veteran whose career seemed to be finished, whom Billy would give one more year. It's messy, putting a team like this together. Every year, however, they compete at the top with all the big dogs.

Billy Beane learned there's always more life left in people than folks are willing to acknowledge. Crawl around in the mud, the dark places, and you will be surprised how much potential still exists among the broken. Hope-filled leaders are always looking for promise and potential even in the midst of pain.

Do you have love for hurting people? Are you the kind of person who sees hope in the midst of impossible situations? Are you willing to take chances on people who are broken? There's a good chance you are a minister among misfits, a messenger to messy people.

twelve

MISFIT EXPECTATIONS

We hear the saying all the time: "Don't get your hopes up." I've never liked that saying. It seems to me that we should be getting our hopes up—and keeping them up all the time. The homeless families who come into the Dream Center fill out a survey when they come in. One of the questions they answer before they move in and receive their free housing is this: "Do you feel safe and secure right now?" We have found that only 2 percent say they felt safe before they moved into the Dream Center.

They also answer the same question before they move out. The response to the same question has been 100 percent positive. This is absolutely staggering to me, yet not surprising. Only 2 percent said they feel safe before coming in, but afterward, 100 percent feel safe. Sounds to me like some families are getting their hopes up.

Our expectations must not fit the mold of this world. We must have misfit expectations. If the outside world doesn't look at our hope and say, "That is over the top," then we haven't truly lived yet. Our expectations for what life can be for anyone who calls upon the name of the Lord should be off the charts. The miracle stories of misfits who became dreamers are not just for a select few in the Bible; they are a standard for what our lives can become.

The world will often try to label people who truly believe God can do anything *weird, strange,* or even *idealistic.* When we stepped out in faith to buy this $3.9 million hospital in 1997 with no money, we were called every name in the book. Some called us *reckless.* Others called us destined to fail. When we first came to Los Angeles, one guy told us, "You won't last long—this city is a graveyard for pastors."

Not long ago, a pastor of a famous church wanted to meet with me about starting a church in Los Angeles. It was a big ministry with global impact. The first thing that comes to mind when someone like that comes to your city is, "Protect your turf." The pastor announced he was coming to Los Angeles and my mind went back twenty years.

I could remember the people who told us that what we wanted to do was impossible. It really discouraged us. I looked at that pastor and decided to speak great things over his life. I told him the doors of this city were wide open to experience revival. I want that church to look back one day and realize they'd had people pulling for them since the beginning.

Great expectations are the breeding ground for miracles. If we believe God is a great God, we will believe for great things. I'm sad to admit it, but when I first started to pastor, I feared failure so much that I actually looked for excuses to fail. I was so occupied with the thought of failure that I would focus more on creative excuses than great expectations. For instance, if people didn't come it was because we didn't have enough parking. Then I realized I was living with a victim mind-set. I had been surrendering to the idea that losing was my only option before even playing on the field.

We fear too much. We're afraid of old age, recession, cancer, war, disease, and unemployment, and some even fear the return of seventies music. And it's really silly. There's a staggering verse in the Bible, when Job said, "For the thing which I greatly feared is come upon me" (Job 3:25 KJV). Does it mean Job was afraid he would lose his donkeys, oxen, camels, and wealth? I don't really know. Does it mean Job feared he would lose his children? Does it mean that once he lost one thing, then he feared losing something else?

1. You will be tormented until you face fear.

I believe that fear feeds off one thing and multiplies. The minute we give in to little fears, they reproduce. At thirty-eight years of age I had trouble breathing and it caused me to have blood clots on both of my lungs, known as a pulmonary embolism. It's a life-threatening thing that blocks your ability to breathe.

Because of this pulmonary embolism, I was terrified to

do anything that had to do with breathing. I would run and be afraid that I would be unable to breathe. My fear of what happened was preventing me from living the best years of my life. Finally, I decided that although I was healed of it, I wasn't healed on the inside until I did something extreme. Two years after my pulmonary embolism, I told the church I was going to run the LA marathon. How did I respond to my greatest fear? By stepping up to the greatest challenge. The ultimate test.

Yes, I was fearful in training and couldn't sleep weeks before the marathon. I will never forget the joy that swept over me during the race, but then the wall hit. The eighteen- to twenty-four-mile stretch. The hardest thing I've ever faced. That six-mile stretch taught me everything I needed to know about perseverance.

I started to think about all the things that could go wrong. Then I stopped myself and said, "Don't let fear multiply; you've come this far, go all the way." It was the most difficult and yet liberating experience of my life. I decided this victory would be the launching pad to crushing fear. The finish line wasn't just an end to the race—it was the end to this torment of fear. Once I faced this fear, it has never reared its ugly head again.

2. Fear creates barriers bigger than they really are.

Fear highlights the boundaries rather than the possibilities. Fear desires that we continue to build up the wall of doubt until our lives become one great obstacle and fear lurks around every corner. Fear wants to become a monument in our lives, when the truth is it should be treated like an unwelcome guest.

I recently took my daughter to Universal Studios here in Los Angeles, and we went on the tram ride. The tram takes you through some of Hollywood's famous movie sets. We turned the corner and came to the famous house from the movie *Psycho*. The actual house in the horror movie. They added a little twist to it. They had a man who looked like the character Norman Bates walk out of the house with a knife and act as if he was coming after the train. I had been on that train several times and never saw that coming.

My little daughter saw it and it terrified her. She couldn't sleep that night. When I tried to put her to bed she said, "Dad, I was fearing the man with the knife, but now I'm fearing the shark from *Jaws* that came out of the water, and now I'm afraid of King Kong too. Oh, Dad, help me! I'm afraid of everything."

One fear brought on another fear. Before long, fear becomes a pattern and a dwelling place in our spirits. I used to fear everything about the city of Los Angeles. I used to look at those high-rise buildings as intimidating giants. Twenty years later, I look at those same buildings as a symbol of a city that has become my refuge. How did I get to that place? I made a decision to start loving the things I feared.

There were certain streets in my city that I used to be afraid of—Temple Street, for instance. So I started to pray for Temple Street, tried to love Temple Street, and drove around at night and visualized making a difference there. I could not fear the things I chose to love.

A great reversal began to take place. Encouraged, I took out a map of my city and picked street after street to pray for, and for which I would believe God for great things. The amazing thing is, the streets I used to be terrified to even walk are now the same streets where I have zero fear. "Perfect love drives fear away."

The reason crime has dropped in our community in such an amazing way is that we've made the transformation from fearing our community to loving it. Loving our community has caused us to be inspired to produce action, solve problems, believing there's something greater around every corner.

When love drives out fear, life becomes an open door.

Maybe you fear a marriage falling apart. Choose instead to fall in love all over again with the person you are married to. Skid Row used to be a terrifying place in my life until one day I decided to live homeless right on the streets of Skid Row until I stopped fearing it. Two days later, after sleeping in the cold Los Angeles night, a great transition took place. I no longer feared Skid Row; I started to love the people there.

Many of the men who come to the Dream Center in rehab arrive straight from prison. They come to this place and are often told they have to stay in the same area as someone they used to fight in prison. How can these men coexist? Love! They were forced to be in a position where they could either kill each other or apply the Word they had received in Bible study and learn to love each other.

We are called to have great expectations in this life. Our expectations for people, for life, ought to not fit into the world's skepticism. People can change, and anything is possible, because God is in everything.

We really believe our community can change, and many think we are crazy. But we are proud to carry the label of people with unrealistic expectations. Let me tell you about another miraculous misfit member of our staff. Her name is Cassandra, and she runs our mobile food bank that feeds tens of thousands of people a week. That's not a typo. We sometimes feed up to thirty thousand people a week.

Cassandra's is an extraordinary story of grace and a prime example that people can still believe God for great things despite the torment of yesterday. When a misfit becomes activated in faith, they often have no idea that limitations are even there. The joy in being a part of God's plan ignites a fire in their souls to do something great. Cassie found that passion in the midst of her pain. Here is her story.

My name is Cassandra Demman, and I am currently the director of the food truck ministry at the Dream Center. I came to the Dream Center on April 15, 2008, for the women's discipleship program.

I was raised in Ironwood, Michigan, by loving Christian parents. I am the sixth of eight kids, with three older sisters I looked up to. Two went to Christian colleges in Tulsa, and the oldest went to a local university.

I spent a summer with my oldest sister when I was thirteen and was introduced to drinking. When I went home, I started to look at Christianity as just a bunch of rules and fun that I couldn't have.

By the time I was fifteen, I was a pothead and an alcoholic. I entered into a relationship after high school that became abusive and was centered on drugs. I finally left him after eight years and began to use more frequently to deal with what had happened. I became a blackout drinker, mixing any kind of pills I could with alcohol.

I came to Los Angeles to visit my other sister when she had her first baby and was introduced to Angelus Temple, the church at the Dream Center. Shortly after that visit, she sent me an application for the discipleship program. I knew Jesus was the answer to my struggle, and I was finally ready to humble myself and get the help I needed.

When I arrived, I was overwhelmed with a sense of peace and joy. I knew I was no longer going to be just someone who believed in God, but someone who was going to completely surrender to His will in my life.

I learned so much in my first year of discipleship that I could feel God calling me to stay for another. I served as a resident advisor my second year, and was able to encourage other women to grow closer to the Lord and fall in love with the Word.

In my third year, Pastor Caroline asked me to take over the food truck ministry. I was scared, but I wanted to allow God to continue to work in my life and develop leadership skills that were only possible with His help. I have been serving as the director for over three years now and have enrolled in Angelus Bible Institute's Bible school.

I also met my wonderful husband at the Dream Center, and we are expecting our first child together in February. The Dream Center has completely changed my life, and I am forever grateful for Pastors Matthew and Caroline believing in me and allowing me to see God's plan unfold in my life.

Belief is a powerful thing. Usually when an organization makes a comeback, it's because a feeling of belief was restored. The crowds began to swell around Jesus because He spoke a language that was uncommon—you could call it misfit language. Jesus spoke of faith moving mountains, and all things being "possible to him who believes" (Mark 9:23 NASB). He didn't just speak these declarations of great expectations to be positive; He did it to affirm people that something bigger was going on—that the God of creation was alive and moving.

Defeat after defeat can create a belief system that says, "I wonder what trouble lurks around the corner?" or "When is the other shoe going to drop?" Instead, why don't we seek God, wake up, and say, "I wonder what great thing You will do today." Living in fear can prevent us from enjoying a current season of victory because we fear a reversal. I'm not saying bad things don't happen. They do. But even if they do occur, if you have high expectations, you will be wired to see the possibilities even in setbacks.

The storms make us stronger.

The beautiful thing about God is He usually exceeds our expectations and does things that leave us shaking our heads in disbelief. I walk around the Dream Center campus and see almost every department being run by someone who went through our recovery program. Here's the incredible thing: most of the time I forget they went through our program. The transformation is so remarkable that I do not even recognize the old person anymore. They work in major departments, they are sharp, they are professional, and they exceed our wildest expectations.

In Ephesians 3:20, the Bible describes "him that is able to do exceeding abundantly above all that we ask or think, according to the power that worketh in us" (KJV). I used to think that scripture was a good Bible bookmarker quote. Now I realize it's a reality.

In Philippians 1:6, Paul said, "I am confident of this very thing, that He who began a good work in you will perfect it until the day of Christ Jesus" (NASB).

It's one thing to believe God for great things when everything is just starting; it's another thing to continue to believe God will carry it out. Whatever God starts, He's going to finish. A life of great expectations is an ongoing process. This is why Paul and Silas could praise God in the middle of their prison (Acts 16). Their expectation was not in what they could see, but rather in Christ in them.

A confident person sees God in the continuing cycle of what God is perfecting. We can't give up on people with problems or addictions, because God is not done moving.

■

How many of you have gone through the agony of losing weight? I remember when I started to walk and run to lose weight. I was 225 pounds and really wanted to get into shape. I would look at that treadmill like it was my enemy. I would walk and run on that thing for an hour, and I felt so discouraged.

How is this helping? I'm not even going anywhere. I felt like a hamster running in place. I'm the kind of guy who likes to move in a direction! At the end of each run, I would look at the computer screen to see how many calories I had burned. My reward for that work was to see that number on the screen.

A lot more was going on than I thought. Things were happening, even if it felt like I was running in place. It's the same with life. Continue to have great expectations even when it feels like you're going nowhere. Something amazing could be going on that only time will reveal.

Motivated and excited, I continued with my exercise plan and didn't think about getting down to the ideal weight—just about making better choices every day and picking myself up when I made a bad one. I refused to think weight goals, and just started to see life in terms of twenty-four-hour victories. One win at a time.

It's great to have a big vision, but sometimes you have to set little goals on the way to the big goal to keep you moving toward the finish line. Having great expectations for the day ahead allows you to be one day closer to the end goal.

I see it every day. A person comes into the Dream Center with the expectation of just getting clean. In the beginning, that's all they can see in terms of success. They get a few days of trusting God under their belt, then weeks, then years, and then one day they are literally transforming the world in which they live. You can't even recognize them anymore because of the total makeover that comes from a life of great expectations.

When I pull into the parking structure at Angelus Temple where I speak weekly, I always see a beautiful young lady named Laura. Her smile lights up the place, and hers is the perfect first face to welcome you to the Dream Center. I know her story. Her family abandoned her on a vacation to California. Listen to Laura's story, and witness the amazing transformation of another one of our staff members.

When I was about nine years old, my mom got married to a man my brother and I didn't know. My brother ended up getting kicked out because he didn't agree with the marriage and started acting out. A few years into the marriage, my stepdad started to come into my room late at night. That really messed with my head. I had no idea what was going on—I just knew I didn't like it and wanted it to end.

I started to smoke weed at first, then turned to pills, and even medicine if it got me high. When I told my mom what was going on, he called me a liar and every other name in the book. After that I don't remember ever feeling safe in my own home again.

In the summer we went on vacation to California, but little did I know that I was going to end up staying in California and never going back home. The night we were supposed to go back, my stepdad beat me so severely that I ended up in the hospital. When I woke up, I was surrounded by police officers and a social worker. The social worker was there to tell me that my mom and stepdad had gone back home and left me in California. That's how I ended up in the foster care system.

In my first foster home, I would cry myself to sleep every night. One day one of the girls in the home asked me if I wanted to stop crying. I said yes, and that's when I was introduced to crystal meth. It took over my life. I felt nothing and I cared about no one—I no longer cried. I started to sell drugs and party all the time. I ran away from group homes and foster homes, not caring what would happen to me. I even ended up dropping out of high school.

When I was nineteen, I met a Christian guy. When he found out about my drug addiction, he started to talk to me about God. I ended up breaking up with him, but for some reason he didn't give up on me. He would call me every day and he even gave his pastor my number. I finally answered one of the pastor's calls, and he invited me to his church. I had never spoken to a pastor before but couldn't say no, so I ended up going. I would have to go high, because I would stay up all night and needed something to keep me up all day.

One day I was in church and it was Testimony Night. People were talking about a God who had changed their lives and how they were happy, and I knew I wanted what they had. I ended up telling my pastor everything that was going on in my life and how I was ready to give it all up. He told me about the Dream Center's discipleship program that helps you get back on track.

I did it. It was the hardest thing I ever had to do in my life, but with that God has brought restoration to my family. I had a chance to get my GED, and God has also placed a dream in my heart to work with the children in the foster care system. My life has changed drastically, and I will never turn back.

What a story of hope.

There is potential in people whom society would label misfits. Instead of looking at people as victims with nothing to offer, try telling them that great things are still attainable. Confront people with the possibilities of achieving great things. After you wipe the tears in people's eyes, light a charge in their spirits.

If people can't understand your positive expectations for humanity, then you are probably a misfit. You have misfit expectations compared to the skepticism of the age in which we live. Can I encourage you to never lose that? Stay a misfit and keep your expectations high. Life tries to steal away our childlike passion and transform us into robotic skeptics who live life seeing the bad in everything. Don't let it happen.

■

One of the girls in our program was a sixteen-year-old runaway. When she came to us, she came as a cutter. She would stab herself daily in order to relieve the pain that was going on in her mind. Cutters have so much mental turmoil that they torture their own bodies as an outlet for their torment. Here she was, a sixteen-year-old cutter, living under a bridge in Lomita, California.

She was a blackout drinker and was so dirty and filthy that they wouldn't let her into retail stores. Left only with a small bottle of hand sanitizer, this teenage girl woke up one day covered in sewer water. She used that small bottle of sanitizer to clean her entire body. She cried out for help, and her mom sent her here to the Dream Center. She arrived homeless, a cutter, bulimic, and emotionally dead.

When she shares her testimony, she does so on two levels. She talks about how life was out there surviving as a homeless teen. You can see pain that comes from talking about it, but then gears shift and she utters my two favorite words: *but then.* "But then I came to the Dream Center and God got ahold of my life, and now I have a dream to one day be a minister."

Her eyes light up and the smile returns. Embracing Jesus is not just a place of refuge, but a place of renewed expectation. My advice to you is to get your expectations up—way up—as high as you can, and just see how He will respond.

AFTERWORD

CARRYING CHRIST'S LOVE TO MISFIT PLACES

P astor, will you come and speak at the Whisky night-club on Sunset Boulevard?" a voice asked over the line. I almost dropped the phone. *The Whisky?* The same place on the Sunset Strip that produced almost every famous heavy metal band? Bands like Mötley Crüe and Poison got their start at the Whisky a Go-Go nightclub. The request was almost humorous.

I get requests all the time to speak at church conferences and even business events, but the Whisky on a Friday night was one for the ages. I found out that one of our Christian heavy metal bands, who called themselves Under the Influence, bought time to play on a Friday night. They bought the time so they could use it the way they wanted to. They said, "Pastor, can you give an altar call at the end of the metal concert? We want you to invite people to come to Christ."

That Friday our heavy metal band took the stage and did their series of songs. Then, after earning the respect of the crowd and establishing that they were a legit band, they went into a set of songs that glorified God. Shaking, terrified, sick to my stomach, the last thing I wanted to do was to take the stage. *How do you preach at the Whisky? What do you say? Should I even be at this place talking about Jesus?* I thought.

My entire life I'd been taught that nightclubs were evil. I had no sermon, no plan, and I was clearly removed from the safe confines of a church service. While writing this book, I wished I could go back to that time in the late nineties and find out what I actually said that night. To my surprise, I discovered someone had posted a clip from that night, preserving that short sermon.

You know, I was walking down the street and found out there is a drug out in the market right now that's the most powerful drug in the world. This drug is on the street right now, and it's doing something to people all over this world. But I want to tell you something tonight: I've become addicted to this drug. It's called being drugged up by the touch of the Holy Spirit of God in our lives. It's not the kind of drug that has you going to bed at night and waking up in the morning singing sad songs. It's the kind of drug that when you get up in the morning, you feel like you want to make a difference in this generation, because we were born to live.

This generation was not born to be a Generation X, sitting home depressed and tired and writing sad songs. This is a generation that's been made to take over and take control of their future. If you feel tonight that you're scared and left all alone, tonight you can come up to any one of us and we will pray for you right there. We will take you in at our center. We will love you. We will believe in you.

We wouldn't want anybody praying for us who wouldn't fight for us, so we will fight for you to. 'Cause, man, we love you. I'm a twenty-three-year-old pastor. I've never tried drugs or alcohol in my life, but I do know one thing. When I was five years old I accepted Christ, and I got the biggest high of my life and I've been serving him ever since.

Tonight if you feel alone or scared, the drug you need is Jesus Christ, dead and resurrected to forgive you and save you and give you a brand-new chance. If you feel alone, that chance is right here tonight after this final song. Will you come and pray with us after? We will lay hands on you and believe for a miracle.

Looking back, I can see this wasn't the perfect sermon. Being available doesn't always mean being perfect; it just means being available. After the sermon was over, shockingly, there was a good response. People asked me questions about Jesus and how to find this drug. I began to tell them it was theirs for free and to tell the story of the saving power of Christ.

Taking the gospel to misfit places is the ultimate rush. It forces us to live outside our circumstances and controlled element. Every strategy of carrying the gospel to unfamiliar places might not involve preaching a sermon at a nightclub, but it does require courage. Many churches are afraid of asking people to come to Jesus even at their own church services. That's because we don't want to offend anyone. If that's such a barrier in our churches, how much more of a barrier it must be outside in our communities. We have good news, but why is it so hard to share?

Sometimes carrying the gospel to obscure places isn't a sermon like I gave at the Whisky; it's a lifestyle of good works that causes people to stop in their tracks and wonder what motivates us to do these things. One day some people in our church got excited to serve. A division of our Adopt-a-Block program is called Random Acts of Kindness—people just thinking outside of the box about crazy ways in which to serve. We adopted a gas station back when the price of gas was soaring. For an hour the gas prices at that station were slashed nearly in half.

People couldn't figure out what was happening. They pulled into the station and found out the people from the Dream Center were paying down the gas prices that hour. People thought it was too good to be true. People from the Dream Center were pumping people's gas and handing them a much cheaper gas bill. Cars began to pile up, and the people asked questions about why we would do something like that. It opened a door for us, right there in the gas station, to share what inspires us to serve: a relationship with Jesus.

The gospel, the message of Christ, was made to go where it doesn't traditionally fit in. It's interesting that almost every story we love about the works and ministry of Jesus involves things that happened outside a building of worship. Yet we often focus on what happens in a church building. The message of Christ is lived out through the transformation of His people. Sunday morning church is not the destination spot for the church but the launching pad of inspiration for what we can be and do Monday through Saturday.

God has placed you somewhere you have unique influence to share His love. Yes, *you*. You have influence somewhere that no one else has. My advice is to live intentionally about your influence and be confident in the One who loves you and the power your influence could have in the lives of others. Don't worry if you don't have it all together; there's value in your vulnerability. Carry God's love to misfit places.

When I think of Jesus walking this earth, healing the sick, and forgiving people of sins, I always visualize people who self-appointed themselves to be the keepers of Jesus' agenda. People thought Jesus was going to set things in order and conquer the world through power, and they had to be frustrated that Jesus would not go and do what they wanted Him to do.

I can imagine an advisory team trying to direct Jesus on where to go and what to do next, but Jesus would go out of His way to bring His message to off-the-path places. In the political world, a candidate will go to the places that give him the best chance of winning an election. Jesus would continually go out of His way to seek out people who could do nothing to maximize His short time of public ministry.

This is why I love Jesus. (Well, that and many other reasons too.) He sought people out to love, and went out of His way to do it. People had to have scratched their heads when Jesus ministered to the divorced woman by the well, or when Jesus forgave the woman caught in the act of adultery, or when He ate dinner with crooked tax collectors. *This isn't what we had in mind when we visualized a conquering Messiah*, they must have thought. *Why in the world is He hanging out with those folks? These people can do nothing to advance our mission.*

Looking back at the Bible, those inspiring encounters minister so far beyond Jesus' walk on earth. He wasn't about getting approval votes; He was out to set an example that would inspire people for generations. It's not always what we accomplish in life, but what we set in motion that really contains influence.

As a pastor, I attend a lot of funerals. Even in memorials honoring influential people, the things said about that person are fascinating for one reason. Even if a person accomplishes great things or moves the masses, the praise usually heaped upon them is more about who they were rather than what they did.

What we do is important, but who we are lives on.

■

My grandfather was the most childlike man I've ever met. He was one of the first pastors ever to lead a church of one thousand back when that was considered a megachurch. My grandfather, Herschel Barnett, did not like going to the office. His beautiful, classy wife, Joy, took care of that. He didn't even like to prepare sermons. In fact, one day when I was visiting his church, he told the church he didn't have a sermon yet. He asked for five more minutes and for the choir to sing one more song while he finished his message onstage. The man was a riot!

Nearly all his sermons were drawn from his real-life experiences as a man who walked up and down his city loving people. He was a street minister who just so happened to pastor a big church. He would hang out with the guys at the tattoo parlor and walk into bars; there was no place his feet would be afraid to go. He believed sharing the gospel and spreading joy were as natural as breathing. He was a walking magnet to Jesus.

Because he believed the gospel belonged in misfit places, there was never a sense of fear anywhere he went. He freely gave away his money. He loved the homeless men in his city, and they all knew him by name. He supported his local schools and was called "the preacher."

I should add that street ministry is not always easy. I like to say that street ministry is the only place where someone can cuss you out and thank you within five minutes and mean it both times.

One day my grandfather decided that on vacation he was going to drive from Kansas City, where he lived, all the way to Mexico, just to hand out bags of candy he had saved for months. He would drive down to pass out candy to the children and then drive back.

Places were never afraid of "the preacher" coming into their establishments because they knew he loved Jesus, and they knew he would do anything for them. He earned the right to be heard in their lives. Some accepted Christ; some did not. They might have rejected his position on Christ, but they never rejected Christ because of the preacher's disposition.

When he died, he had a stunning funeral. All the city's homeless showed up along with public officials and the toasts of the town. The church was packed about fifty-fifty with the elite and the poor. Fighting for misfits is not always easy. You will lose people in your church because some will get weary of the message to love the hurting. It's natural for humans to look inward and ask, *What's in it for me?* But stay the course and welcome misfits.

Include everyone into the basic philosophy of how you live your life. In your family life, get involved in a lifestyle of helping whosoever. Teach your kids to look for the unpopular in their schools and to welcome them. We must educate our families that going with the flow isn't always right. Living for God's Word will often be against the flow. Find ways to bring your family into the life of serving. Even if they protest and want to stay home and play video games, encounters of serving will change their lives.

■

It can get very hot during the summer in Los Angeles. Ramona Gardens is a housing project located in East Los Angeles where we have been serving for fifteen years. One day the police approached two of the committed people who serve at that project site because they were concerned that the kids were breaking fire hydrants to cool off from the sun. This was costing the city too much money. The police asked the two Adopt-a-Block leaders if they had any solutions.

The team met with the kids and asked them why they were breaking fire hydrants. The kids explained they had never been to a water park before and were just having fun. The leaders responded by saying they did not have enough money to take the kids to a water park, but they could create their own water park at home. The Adopt-a-Block team made a homemade Slip'N Slide with Hefty trash bags, stakes, and dish soap. The kids had a blast!

About a month later, the police realized the kids in Ramona Gardens had not broken a single fire hydrant since that day. A local police officer patrolling the projects pulled over to say thank you to one of the leaders. He chuckled at the creative idea that had made such a difference. The homemade water park really influenced those kids. The things we find ourselves creating for others can make us laugh sometimes!

Another young lady in the church had an idea so simple that it was shocking how well it worked. She started a Bible school pedicure class on the grass lawn in the Ramona Gardens housing project. Young girls received nail painting and pedicures before the Bible study. They loved the "pedicure Bible club." For them, it was the event of a lifetime.

I attended the class and the little girls practically tackled me and then started to paint my nails. This was the first and only time I allowed someone to paint my nails. The girls held me hostage with their adorable smiles and went to work on my feet. Then the Bible instructor, in her lovely Australian accent, talked about Jesus on that grass lawn, and the girls were captivated. Carrying Christ to others is a lifestyle.

Compassion is like deodorant: you've got to put it on every day. How many times do we hear in the Bible that Jesus was moved with compassion? (Matt. 14:14, 20:34; Mark 1:41, 6:34). We have to put ourselves in situations that force us to be moved. Can I be honest for a second? I'm a work in progress. When the Bible says, "all our righteous acts are like filthy rags," I get it (Isa. 64:6).

Many times I don't feel that I'm living up to my potential in the area of compassion. Selfishness is a very easy place for me to visit, and at times even linger. I've got to force myself to see the need and then it reactivates compassion. Selfishness comes easily when we stay locked up in our own world. I have to leave my office and walk around the Dream Center campus to remind myself that it's about others.

The greatest energy boost we can get comes from carrying compassion to people who are hurting. We live in a world that is constantly looking for ways to get energy. How many of you have stood behind a person at Starbucks who orders a triple shot? Or someone who buys cases of energy drinks? But take it from me: serving produces chemical-free energy. Spiritual energy.

We all need energy to deal with our burdens, both physical and otherwise. The Bible says in Matthew 11:28–30,

> Come to me, all you who are weary and burdened, and I will give you rest. Take my yoke upon you and learn from me, for I am gentle and humble in heart, and you will find rest for your souls. For my yoke is easy and my burden is light.

You mean when you come to Christ and give Him your burden, you still have a burden? Yes, Jesus gives you a new burden. The good news is that the burden He gives you is light, because it's a burden of emptying, not accumulating. The reason your burden is so heavy is because you are constantly adding to it and picking up pain along the pathway of life. When you lay your burden down, Christ gives you a new one.

This burden is different. You are loving in spite of your pain, you are serving out of your conflict, and the burden is light because you are emptying yourself instead of adding. Inward living produces outward devastation. Outward serving produces inner joy. His load is light because it's a load of giving. Unloading your burden is the best way to see energy restored to your life.

■

Writing this book has been fascinating. When I write books I like to write them in public places. Much of this book has been written at an IHOP. The sounds in the background in public places fascinate me. While I'm working, I can hear arguments, conversations, and sometimes people fighting over the bill.

Most of the arguments I hear involve people wanting to prove they are right about something. An older man at the table next to me is cussing at those "crooked politicians." You learn a lot about life just hearing people talk about what they want in life, and what would make them happy.

We want and want and want, and there's always an empty feeling when what we get is not enough. Serving has never left me empty, but always filled. I have found the more time I have to look inside myself, the more time I have to feel cheated, victimized, and self-centered. I'm not different from the people here at the International House of Pancakes. The thing I've got going for me is that I know what to do when life becomes all about me: jump into someone else's need.

The disciples argued about who was the greatest, who would get the best seats in the kingdom (Luke 9:46). Whenever something like that happened, Jesus responded by placing a child in their midst or telling them to look at the fields that were "white already to harvest" (John 4:35 KJV). Jesus' response was to look outward. He was trying to tell them that you can't carry your burden and Jesus' burden at the same time. Serving is not always a strategy, an idea; it's a way of life. It's a way of treating people—a way of encouraging.

The other day I was at a Jack in the Box drive-through making such a huge order that I felt bad about laying it on the person inside. I went to the window, and the lady was beaming with joy. I apologized for the big order, and the lady said, "Sir, it's such an honor to take that big order."

I said, "You are a nice person. Thank you."

"God has been so good to me, and serving people like you makes my day," she replied.

Never had anyone said that to me at a drive-through! How can a lady be so happy working that often thankless job? She decided to serve right there where she was with a good attitude.

That lady made an impression on me for a lifetime. The size of her paycheck did not determine the size of her joy. Her joy was in being a joy peddler at that drive-through window. Jesus shined through her long before she even said, "God gave me this honor to serve." When someone serves with joy, it really does demonstrate beautiful Christian behavior. Radical compassion—what a beautiful thing.

Carrying the compassion of Christ is not confined to a building-a-ministry idea, a building, or a million-dollar facility. It's bigger than that. You can't carry a building everywhere you go, but you can bring yourself, and you are a gift to the world. I constantly challenge myself with the idea that the Dream Center is not a building where compassion happens, but a lifestyle in which to live. We carry the compassion of

Christ all the time, everywhere. We are all moving Dream Centers, igniting dreams through the love of Jesus Christ.

Carry compassion everywhere you go, in every situation. May our lives be a reflection of beautiful compassion.

■

My wife was a volunteer at the Dream Center. She has served here as a missionary since she was eighteen years of age, driving back and forth a total of three hours every day just so she could work at the Dream Center. She gave her life for missions in Los Angeles. We've mentioned the story about how she started the mobile food truck and its impact on the city. Caroline knows the problems and needs of this city better than any person I know. We dated for only three months before we got married. What can I say? When you know, you know.

I wanted to surprise her with the marriage proposal and do something dramatic that would be worthy of the incredible person she is. I called a pastor friend and asked if he could produce a fake letter inviting her out to New York to speak at his church about her food truck ministry. We were dating at the time, and she came running into my office with the letter saying, "I've been invited to speak at my first church service!"

I wanted to laugh but had to be cool to keep my perfect plan in place. She said, "Will you help me with my sermon?"

I thought, *Well, that was extra work I wasn't expecting in this plan.* I helped her to prepare a sermon she would never preach. She received her fake flight itinerary from the church and the ticket I had purchased.

She asked if I could take her to the airport at eight o'clock the next morning for her flight. I couldn't take her because I was leaving at 6:00 a.m. to carry out my plan of proposal. I had to get there first. I said, "Can someone else take you? It's quite early in the morning." She was shocked at my response. She probably thought I was the worst boyfriend ever.

She found someone to take her to the airport. When she landed in New York City, a driver from the church picked her up and said, "Can I take you on a little tour of New York before you speak tomorrow?" Caroline was very excited to see the city. She had never been there, and the city can take your breath away the first time you see it. The driver was a perfect actor as part of my scheme. She said, "I would love to take you to the Empire State Building."

Little did Caroline know I was already at the top of the observation deck sweating bullets, trying to rehearse the perfect proposal. Every time an elevator opened, I thought Caroline would get off. Dozens of elevators stopped and dropped off passengers as I waited two hours at the top of that deck. Finally, the one opened up with Caroline inside. My head spun in circles, and the world went into slow motion.

I grabbed her by the hand, took her to the best spot on the deck, got on my knee, and asked her to marry me in front of tourists from all over the world. I had a lot of support from the crowd. People were saying, "Yes! Say yes!" (I needed all the support I could get). She didn't say yes at first. She just hugged me.

When she finally did say yes, that was not just a turning point in our personal love life, but a commitment to our love affair with the people of Los Angeles and the cause of carrying compassion to everyone.

Here's the beautiful side of the story. My wife wanted to plan the wedding in a way that reflected our life and our values. I let her plan the wedding, because every man knows that's a good idea. She said, "Pastor Matthew . . ." (I'm not kidding you—she was so used to calling me "pastor" as a volunteer that it took her awhile to drop that salutation.) "Can we bring in all the homeless, the families that I serve in the community, to the wedding?"

How cool is that? My wife wanted to bring the homeless to the wedding. Sounds like a parable in the Bible, doesn't it? We now had an unexpected budgetary item added to the wedding: bus rental for the homeless. You don't see that every day. Nearly two thousand people showed up to our outdoor wedding. We had the general manager of the Dodgers at the wedding and the great singer Lou Rawls sang at the service.

The contrast between celebrities and the homeless was extremely obvious and beautiful. When the wedding was over, neighborhood taco trucks showed up to feed the visitors street tacos. My wife is an expert designer and a fashion specialist, yet she invited everyone to join the biggest day of her life, even if it wasn't magazine glossy. She wanted serving to be a lifestyle and incorporated it into every part of her life. It was a beautiful misfit wedding. I knew that day that life lived with her was going to be a wonderful life full of adventures.

Paul told the church that we are living epistles (2 Cor. 3:2). We are living love letters to this world. We live, move, and love in a way the world cannot understand but gladly embraces. We have so many encounters in this world. We marry, we bury, we shop, we take our kids to school. Moving about the daily affairs of your life, carry compassion with you.

You might feel ordinary, but don't let that disqualify you from being used by God. You might have misfits around you, but don't let that stop you from lending a helping hand. Whether you feel like a misfit or you are trying to reach misfits, in God's kingdom all misfits are welcome.

ACKNOWLEDGMENTS

I would like to take some time to thank some very special people in my life. People who have inspired me to love more, serve more, and who have brought great meaning to my life.

My wife, Caroline: The woman who showed me that loving people is not an occasional event but a lifestyle. All these years being married she's never stopped loving the biggest of all . . . me. You inspire me every single day to love with foundational sincerity and to do everything from the heart. I love you!

Caden: My wonderful son whose life is a gift every single

day. A young man whose calm spirit and funny sense of humor make me anticipate the hours daily just to be near him.

Mia: My adventurous daughter who will drop everything to do the spontaneous thing and who keeps her old dad feeling young. You are every daddy's dream.

My mother, Marja. You are such a strong woman who can make up her mind to do anything. So full of fun, perseverance, and perfectly unconventional. You've always loved the underdog. You live the message of embracing misfits.

Luke. My older brother who now I call best friend. What a role model you are!

Kristie. The loyal big sister who makes me smile just thinking about her zeal for life.

My father, Tommy. The biggest dreamer I've ever known. Yet, your ambition has always been healthy and it's been for others' well-being. A man who has sacrificed it all for the sake of others and has done it for no other reason except to honor God.

My assistant Todd. Treasures are laid up in heaven for good deeds that have gone unnoticed. You might be the wealthiest man in heaven one day.

My assistant Aaron. You've traveled with me all over this world and you've always found that incredible extra gear to give more. Wow!

My church, Angelus Temple, and the Dream Center. You are the only church I've ever known. Decades I've been your pastor and I've never wanted to be anywhere else. What an incredible honor to pastor a church that isn't afraid to bring misfits into the house of God. In fact, a church that begs to live on the edge and desires to be stretched and challenged to live with greater compassion. Let's keep going!

Thanks to Thomas Nelson for taking a risk on a book like this and seeing the value of the radical call to action.

ABOUT THE AUTHOR

Matthew Barnett is pastor of Angelus Temple and the Dream Center in Los Angeles, California, the first of 150 Dream Centers launched around the world. He is also the best-selling author of *The Church That Never Sleeps* and *The Cause Within You*. Barnett is married with two children.